TOWARDS EFFICIENCY
IN READING

TOWARDS EFFICIENCY
IN READING

TEN PASSAGES FOR PRACTICE
IN FASTER AND MORE EFFICIENT
READING FOR STUDENTS
AND ADULTS

by

GORDON WAINWRIGHT

CAMBRIDGE
AT THE UNIVERSITY PRESS
1968

Published by the Syndics of the Cambridge University Press
Bentley House, P.O. Box 92, 200 Euston Road, London, N.W. 1
American Branch: 32 East 57th Street, New York, N.Y. 10022

© This collection Cambridge University Press 1968

Library of Congress Catalogue Card Number: 68–10690

Standard Book Number: 521 06720 0

Printed in Great Britain
at the University Printing House, Cambridge
(Brooke Crutchley, University Printer)

CONTENTS

ACKNOWLEDGEMENTS

For permission to reproduce copyright material acknowledgement is made to the following: Penguin books Ltd for *Communications* by Raymond Williams, *Personal Values in the Modern World* by M.V.C. Jeffreys and *Discrimination and Popular Culture* by Denys Thompson; The British Broadcasting Corporation and Sir Hugh Greene for 'The BBC's Duty to Society'; The English Universities Press and Simon & Schuster Inc. for *Straight and Crooked Thinking* by Robert Thouless; Pan Books Ltd and Fawcett Publications Inc. for *How to Study* by Harry Maddox; Beacon Press for *Six Days or Forever?* by Ray Ginger; Harper & Row Inc. for *The True Believer* by Eric Hoffer.

INTRODUCTION

Many students in the senior forms in schools, technical colleges and universities, as well as many adults working in a variety of positions in business and industry, are much slower readers than they need be. Their slowness springs, fundamentally, from a lack of flexibility in their approach to the range of reading materials which they encounter. No one would for a moment suggest that, when driving a car, we should drive at a single steady speed—or even a narrow range of speeds—no matter what the road conditions. We all accept that, when driving, we proceed slowly and carefully in a busy city centre, whilst on a motorway where there is little traffic we can afford to drive at a much higher speed. Yet slower readers tend to 'drive' slowly all the time, no matter what the nature of the material or their purpose in reading it. This is quite patently inefficient. Not every piece of reading material, nor every purpose in reading, requires a slow, ponderous approach.

The Nature of Efficiency in Reading

In order to read efficiently, we need to develop a sufficient flexibility in our techniques of reading to allow us to select the most appropriate reading speed for each piece of material. Efficiency in reading may, then, be thought of as reading each individual piece of reading material as quickly as the nature of the material and one's purpose in reading it allow. There is thus no really objective standard by which we can measure efficiency in reading. We cannot say that at a certain speed and a certain level of comprehension efficiency is achieved. It is largely a personal matter and we are each reading efficiently when our speed in reading and the degree of attention we give are such that we understand what the writer is trying to communicate and retain the information we need to retain.

Results of reading efficiency courses show that most readers are capable of at least doubling their reading speed on any one type of material. Thus, at the beginning of a course, whether it is a course of self-instruction or a group course in a college of further education, most readers will be reading material of an average level of difficulty, such as the passages in this book, at about 200–250 words per minute and will be scoring 6·0–7·0 on the Retention Test. At the end of a course, most readers will be reading the same kind of material at 400–500 words a minute and will be scoring 7·0–8·0 on the Retention Test. The figures for easier and for more difficult material will be proportionately higher and lower, respectively, at both the beginning and the end of a course. However, bearing in mind the point that slower readers tend to read slowly all the time no matter what the level of difficulty or their purpose in reading, it is likely that the *total range* of reading speeds for these slower readers at the beginning of a course will be around 100–300 words per minute. At the end of a course (e.g. by the time the last passage in this book is reached), most readers will be capable of speeds of from 100 words per minute for slow, careful, study-type reading to the equivalent of 800–1000 words per minute for rapid skimming, when all that is required is the gist of the author's message or a knowledge of certain specific pieces of information. (An example of the first type of skimming is reading a light novel for the story-line alone; an example of the second is reading a technical or industrial report on a subject one is familiar with for new information of a factual nature.) This increasing flexibility and increasing accuracy in the choice of the most appropriate technique is the sign of increasing efficiency in reading. We should never be misled into thinking that rapid and efficient reading means reading quickly *all the time*, regardless of the material or one's purpose. Nothing could be more foolhardy. The level of difficulty and what it is necessary to comprehend should always be allowed to dictate the choice of approach and technique.

The Need for Efficiency in Reading

The increasing amount of material to be read, in the form of newspapers, journals, reports, correspondence, memoranda and books, means that, especially at work, a leisurely approach such as one would use in reading a good novel is, in terms of man-hours consumed, expensive. It is also wasteful, for not everything requires the same amount of attention and concentration. The increasing variety of most people's reading diets at work, if they are to be kept up-to-date in their grasp of their own and relevant fields of knowledge and experience, means not only that readers have to be more selective but also that they need to be more purposeful and active in their reading. Passive, leisurely reading is as obsolete in the modern world of business and industry as intuitive and rule of thumb procedures in arriving at managerial decisions.

We need to remember that, outside creative self-expression, effective communication depends upon a strong sense of purpose, active involvement, careful planning and a conscious and deliberate flexibility in approach. In reading, the end must dictate the means, as it must in other forms of communication. People who are enslaved by slow reading habits are allowing the means used to dictate what the end result will be. Since the means are restricted in their variety and degree of appropriateness, the result is invariably that the slower reader does not get as much out of his reading as he knows he should be able to.

The Value of Efficiency in Reading

The first benefit which most students on reading efficiency courses report is that their normal, daily reading of newspapers, correspondence, reports and so on takes them much less time than it used to. Once they realize that there is more to reading than being led by the writer word by word and line by line through what he is trying to communicate to them (as drivers used to be led along the highway by a man with a red flag), they are able to make considerable savings in the time spent reading. This additional time can then be devoted to other, probably more important, aspects of their work and thus increase their overall personal efficiency.

Becoming a more efficient reader also means that, where once reading was something of an unpleasant chore, it becomes a satisfying pleasure and one is much more likely to give reading a higher place in leisure activities. The benefits from this are incalculable.

Most students also notice that, because they have become more interested in the *act* of reading, they become more interested in, and more critical of, *what* they read. This new active involvement in reading produces an improved retention of the information a writer is giving because it results in increased attention and concentration. It makes one's approach to material more thoughtful and makes possible a greater *total* understanding of, and insight into, what a writer has to say. The benefits here for students and for those who have, for example, to make executive and policy decisions on the basis of reports submitted to them are considerable.

How to Achieve Efficiency in Reading

Basically, there are only three elements necessary in one's approach to the process of becoming a more efficient reader. The first is a sincere and conscious desire to improve the speed of reading and the level of retention and comprehension. Unless the student really wants to improve and has enough confidence in his abilities to feel he can improve then it is unlikely that he will improve very much. Attitude is important, for any course which tries to improve personal skills can only succeed if the student wants it to.

The second element is practice. It is necessary to practise reading faster and understanding better for about 15–20 minutes a day during a course of instruction and for another 4–8 weeks after the end of a course. After all, even with teenagers, we are trying to change the habits of at least ten years' standing. This cannot be achieved overnight without effort, for sustained and determined work is necessary for permanent success.

The third element is a spirit of competition. Competition not with others but with oneself. This means that each time one of the passages in this book is read, after the first one, and during each practice session, the student must deliberately try to improve upon his previous best performance in both speed and comprehension. Keeping a close watch on progress as revealed by the progress graphs in this book should help in developing the spirit of self-competition.

The Practice Material Used in This Book

This book contains ten passages, each of which is sufficiently long to provide more than a 'sprinting' exercise in reading speed and each of which is accompanied by comprehension questions and recommendations for further reading practice.

The passages are of an average level of difficulty (with the exception of Passages Seven, Eight and Nine, which are a little more difficult), as measured by the Readability Formula recommended by Fry in *Teaching Faster Reading* (C.U.P., 1963), pp. 135–40, and should be well within the reading abilities of all who have had a secondary education.

The themes of the passages are linked, sometimes closely, sometimes not too closely, so that the material not only provides a basis for work in improving reading efficiency for students working on their own and for groups of students under an instructor but also for at least one year's work in English and Liberal/General Studies for students in schools' sixth forms, post-'G1' level courses in colleges of further education and first year university students. In this latter respect, the passages can be used as starting points for a more general and a deeper consideration of the points and issues they raise. For example, the passage from *Six Days or Forever?* by Ray Ginger could lead not only to further consideration of the scientific, religious and social implications of Darwin's Theory of Evolution, but also to the consideration of similar aspects of other ideas from the history of science and technology.

The central theme of the passages, however, is human communication, its uses, techniques and problems. Starting from the general points made about the teaching of English by Raymond Williams in the first passage, we move to a consideration of some aspects of human thought processes, which is where errors and failures in our abilities to communicate effectively have their origin. Passages Three and Four provide examples of what happens when individuals fail to 'think straight'. Passage Five is concerned with reading efficiency and leads into Passage Six, which deals with effective methods of study. Passage Seven takes us away again to the social and ethical aspects of communication problems. Passage Eight makes certain points with regard to the mass media of communication and Passage Nine discusses some of the issues in sound and television broadcasting. Passage Ten returns us to our starting point.

The first and the last passages in this book are taken from the same source and are of a sufficiently similar level of difficulty for readers to be

4

able to compare their achievements on these passages and see how much they have been able to increase their reading speed and improve their retention and other aspects of comprehension.

The Nature of the Comprehension Tests

Experience has shown that tests which only contain questions to test the reader's ability to retain what he has read give an incomplete guide to the effect of increasing reading speed on comprehension. Similarly, tests which also contain questions calling for deduction, interpretation and evaluation, but which call upon the student to mark these in the same 'right or wrong' manner in which retention questions can be marked, are unsatisfactory.

In an attempt to overcome these difficulties, the comprehension questions in this book have been divided into three sections and performance on each section is assessed in a different way. Section A (Retention Tests) asks readers for factual and other information given in the passage and the answers will be either right or wrong when checked against the appropriate answer key at the back of the book. Section B (Understanding and Interpretation) asks for a variety of things such as the main points made by the writer, deductions on the basis of the information given, the drawing of inferences, the meanings of words and terms. Since some answers given will be neither wholly right nor wholly wrong, the reader is asked to calculate his own score after consulting the comments and recommendations in the appropriate section of the answer key. Section C (Discussion and Evaluation) calls for responses from the reader, in the light of what he has read, which cannot be accurately and reliably assessed in any way but which are still useful tests of whether he has comprehended what he has read. Students working under the guidance of a teacher may be able to obtain some idea of the quality of their performance on this section of the Comprehension Test but students working on their own will have to trust to their own judgement or obtain the 'second opinion' of a friend or colleague. It is ironic that some of the most interesting and useful questions on the material have to be treated in this way, but this fact should help readers to realize that *total* comprehension is not an 'all or nothing', 'right or wrong' affair. There is scope for numerous 'correct' understandings of any piece of reading material.

How to Obtain the Best Results from This Book

Students using this book under the guidance of a teacher should proceed through it at the pace and in the manner he prescribes. (Some suggestions for teachers using this book with groups are given at the back of the book.)

Students working on their own should read one passage a week, preferably on the same day of the week and at the same time of day. Each day, between the weekly sessions with the book, the student should spend 15–20 minutes on the practice work recommended at the end of each passage.

For students with a limited amount of time to spare, the book can be worked through in five weeks instead of ten, reading two passages a week. If this is done, the daily practice sessions should be 20–30 minutes in length. In either case, regular daily practice should continue for at least four weeks after completing the book.

After six months, some passages which are least well remembered should be worked through again to obtain some idea of how far the improvements made have been retained. The same kind of follow-up work should be attempted one year after completing the book.

Procedure for Reading the Passages

To reduce the possibilities of unnecessary variations in the results achieved, the passages in this book should be read under as nearly identical conditions each time and in the following manner:

1 Open the book at the appropriate page.
2 Using a stopwatch or a watch with a second hand, start timing and begin reading.
3 Read the passage through once only. Do not read anything twice—this will cause comprehension to drop at first but it will soon improve. (This advice does not apply to the first and last passages, which, as will be seen, should be read as normally as possible.) On each passage after the first, try to read faster and at the same time understand better. When you have finished reading, write down in a notebook the time taken in minutes and seconds (to the nearest five seconds).
4 Answer the Retention (Section A) and the Understanding and Interpretation (Section B) questions at the end of the passage, writing down your answers in your notebook.
5 Check the answers to the Retention and the Understanding and Interpretation questions against the appropriate answer key at the back of the book and convert the time taken to read the passage into words per minute, using this formula:

$$\frac{\text{No. of words in passage}}{\text{Time taken (in seconds)}} \times 60 = \text{words per minute (w.p.m.)}.$$

6 Referring back to the passage, *find* the correct answers to any Retention or Understanding and Interpretation questions which you answered incorrectly. Getting into the habit of doing this helps to improve comprehension skills. (Groups working with an instructor wil be able to ask him for advice if they have any difficulty in locating the answers to Understanding and Interpretation questions; there should be no trouble in locating those parts of the passages which contain answers to Retention questions.)

6

7 Answer the Discussion and Evaluation (Section C) questions, referring back to the passage or re-reading as required and writing the answers down in your notebook. Groups working with an instructor may prefer to discuss some of these questions orally. You should check the answer key for Section C *before* you attempt to answer the questions because the comments here are frequently designed to assist you in answering the questions.

Passage One

As you read the passage which follows, read at a normal, comfortable speed. Do not read more slowly than you would normally read because of the Comprehension Tests which accompany it. Greater concentration and complete attention to the task in hand are better solutions to comprehension problems than slower reading. Read silently and in silence and try to ensure that you will not be disturbed as you read.

On the other hand, do not, at this stage, try to read the passage faster than you would normally read it. If you do, you will not have a reliable idea of your reading speed and level of comprehension in your everyday reading before you begin the process of improvement. As you will compare your performance on Passage One with your performance on Passage Ten, it is important that you read both in the same way.

Turn over and, following the instructions given above, begin reading.

Begin timing.

PASSAGE ONE

from *Communications* by Raymond Williams

We already teach communication, in certain ways, and we also teach some practice and appreciation of the arts. Some of this work is good, but some of it is limited by assumptions taken over from old-fashioned ideas of culture and society, and some of it is even harmful.

Teaching Speech

At the roots of much of our cultural thinking is our actual experience of speech. In Britain the question of good speech is deeply confused, and is in itself a major source of many of the divisions in our culture. It is inevitable, in modern society, that our regional speech-forms should move closer to each other, and that many extreme forms should disappear. But this should be a natural process, as people move and travel and meet more freely, and as they hear different speakers in films, television, and broadcasting. The mistake is to assume that there is already a 'correct' form of modern English speech, which can serve as a standard to condemn all others. In fact 'public-school English', in the form in which many have tried to fix it, cannot now become a common speech-form in the country as a whole: both because of the social distinctions now associated with its use, and because of the powerful influence of American speech-forms. Yet many good forms of modified regional speech are in practice emerging and extending. The barriers imposed by dialect are reduced, in these forms, without the artificiality of imitating a form remote from most people's natural speaking. This is the path of growth. Yet in much speech training, in schools, we go on assuming that there is already one 'correct' form over the country as a whole. Thousands of us are made to listen to our natural speaking with the implication from the beginning that it is wrong. This sets up such deep tensions, such active feelings of shame and resentment, that it should be no surprise that we cannot discuss culture in Britain without at once encountering tensions and prejudices deriving from this situation. If we experience speech training as an aspect of our social inferiority, a fundamental cultural division gets built in, very near the powerful emotions of self-respect, family affection, and local

8

loyalty. This does not mean that we should stop speech training. But we shall not get near a common culture in Britain unless we make it a real social process—listening to ourselves and to others with no prior assumption of correctness—rather than the process of imitating a social class which is remote from most of us, leaving us stranded at the end with the 'two-language' problem. Nothing is more urgent than to get rid of this arbitrary association between general excellence and the habits of a limited social group. It is not only that there is much that is good elsewhere. It is also that, if you associate the idea of quality with the idea of class, you may find both rejected as people increasingly refuse to feel inferior on arbitrary social grounds.

Teaching Writing

Here again we are faced with the problem of a necessary kind of training being limited by old ideas. It is not only that many of us are taught to write in old-fashioned styles. It is also that the forms we are taught often have little to do with the actual writing we need to practise.

In practice speaking, we are often limited to the formal debate or the casual three-minute speech, though neither, as taught, plays much real part in social life. We need to practise, therefore, such forms as the committee discussion, the verbal report, or the detailed questioning of a speech. Similarly, in writing, we need to practise not only the essay, but also the written report, the memorandum and minutes. One of the few common applied forms we now have is the business letter (perhaps not quite so terrible as it was, but still, as it comes through the post, pretty bad). We could do with regular practice in all kinds of correspondence— the letter of protest to the local paper as often as the acknowledgement of your 'kind favour'. We could also do with some practice in writing official forms, not only because so many are unnecessarily difficult, but also because their ordinary social tone is as regularly a kind of licensed bullying as that of the commercial letter is a kind of non-committal crawling. It would be something if we could learn to write to each other, on official or business occasions, in ways compatible with a self-respecting democratic society.

Teaching Creative Expression

Much of the best practice, in speech and writing, is and ought to be of a creative kind. In our junior schools, particularly, we have learned the value of making poems, stories, plays, figures, pictures, models, music, dance. Some of this work is excellent by any standards. Most of it is interesting. But the major limitation now built into this kind of teaching is that it is regarded as a form of play. This means that at a certain age it can be safely dropped, and put away with other childish things.

It is indeed play in the sense that most of us enjoy doing it. But these creative activities are also forms of work: for many adults, the work to which they give their whole lives. It is only the prejudice of a very narrow and early industrial society that the value of these activities is seen as a sort of harmless and indifferent play or therapy. From these activities comes much of man's real society, and they should be given that kind of respect throughout education. In the changes that come with puberty, it is vital that the practice of these activities should be continued, with no setting of 'more real' or 'more practical' work above them. Otherwise there is unnecessary fading, and all the major arts are relegated to the sphere of 'leisure': a separation which in itself makes inevitable, and much deeper than it ever now needs to be, a separation between art and society. Both sides then suffer; the arts because they are seen as marginal and specialized; society because it is limited to economics and administration. It is depressing to think that much of this division is now actively taught and learned in our schools, which at an earlier stage do so much to show how important and satisfying the arts can be to almost everyone.

Teaching Contemporary Arts

The proper extension of creative practice is direct experience and discussion of all the contemporary arts at their best. The difficulty here is the 'Goldsmith assumption': the idea that education has done its work when it has introduced us to a few classic authors. Of course we should get to know as much as we can of our inherited literature. But if we get to know it as a body of 'classics', we may sometimes confirm what is being taught elsewhere: that the arts are separate, in this case separate in time. It is significant how often, when culture is discussed, the idea of the museum is thrown in, often with real resentment.

In literature, to include contemporary work can have the good effect of unmaking the classics and remaking them as novels, poems, and plays. This is especially the case if living writers are invited into the educational process, at all possible stages, to read and talk about their work. Even if we can only get records of people reading their own work, the atmosphere is still quite different. Similarly, we need not confine experience of painting to standard reproductions on the walls of schools and colleges. Many artists would be glad to be invited, and the local exhibition of painting or sculpture, or the building actually designed, discussed, and built in our own town, is always the place to start learning. Already, in music, composers have proved very willing to travel and play and discuss their work. This kind of contact, with creative artists and performers, is important above all because of the spirit it communicates. We should be careful, moreover, not to play safe in these invitations: we should ask many kinds of creator and performer. The deepest danger, now is the external division (pushed by the media, ratified by education) between those arts which are thought of as serious, academic, and old, and those which are experienced as lively, personal, and new. To underwrite this division harms the traditional work and misses the chance of creating real standards in the new. In this respect, such new forms as jazz and the cinema are crucial. Yet for one school performance and discussion of a good contemporary film there seem to be hundreds of visits to films of 'the classics'—versions of Dickens and Shakespeare made respectable by that fact, yet often inferior, as cinema, to new work. And then good new work, as in jazz, is left mixed up in our minds with the bad work which our educational authorities think they are doing their duty by dismissing as inferior, negligible, and even dangerous. The resentment and confusion this causes has never been adequately appreciated. The only way to get some real movement and understanding is to bring in people who have actual standards, from their own work, and can communicate both its quality and its excitement.

1540 words

In your notebook, write down the time taken to read this passage.

Now, before you do anything else, turn over and answer the Retention Test and the Understanding and Interpretation Test.

COMPREHENSION TESTS

A. Retention

Do not refer back to the passage

1 In teaching speech, what mistaken assumption is often made?
2 In teaching speech, what may happen if the idea of quality is associated with the idea of class?
3 Name *two* forms of writing which the writer thinks we need to practise if we are to improve the quality of our writing.
4 Many of us are taught to write in old-fashioned styles. What other reason is given for the generally low standard of written English?
5 What is the major limitation built into the teaching of creative expression?
6 Name *two* of the examples that the writer gives of creative expression.
7 What is the 'Goldsmith assumption'?
8 How can we get some real movement and understanding in teaching contemporary arts?
9 Why does the writer think that, in teaching contemporary arts, contact with creative artists and performers is important?
10 What does the writer think the relegation of the major arts to the sphere of 'leisure' makes inevitable?

B. Understanding and Interpretation

Do not refer back to the passage

Comments on probable answers are given in the appropriate section of the answer key at the back of the book.

1 List the main points made by the writer in this passage.
2 How would you describe the writer's attitude towards the present methods of teaching communication in the English educational system?
3 What are the implications of what the writer says in this passage?
4 What is the writer's opinion of the 'classics'?
5 Explain the following *in your own words*: 'Goldsmith assumption'; the classics; a common culture; 'public-school English'; the 'two-language' problem.

C. Discussion and Evaluation

You may refer back to the passage

1 In what ways is it important for us all to be able to use the language communication skills of reading, writing, listening and speaking effectively?

2 Assess, from your own experience and bearing in mind what you have just read in Passage One, the effectiveness with which English is taught in schools and colleges today.

3 Do dialects have a place in contemporary spoken English?

4 Attempt a critical evaluation of the passage.

5 How far do you agree or disagree with the points the writer makes? Did these agreements or disagreements influence you unduly in answering the last question?

Practice Work

During the next week, as you read your daily newspaper and any other light and fairly easy reading matter, *try* to read it a little faster than you are accustomed to reading it. Carry out this practice for the recommended 15–20 minutes a day. *Every day.*

Passage Two

As you read the following passage try deliberately to increase your reading speed and raise your retention score above the results you recorded for Passage One.

Compete with yourself on all the passages that follow until you receive other instructions.

Refer back to the Introduction to this book if you are not yet familiar with the procedure to be used in timing the reading of these passages and answering the comprehension questions.

As you read, do not regress (i.e. go back to read something twice). You may find that comprehension suffers at first but that it will soon recover and will probably begin to improve.

PASSAGE TWO

from *Straight and Crooked Thinking* by Robert Thouless

We tend to think wrongly not so much because we do not know the laws of logic as because there are obstacles in our own minds which make us unwilling to think straight on certain subjects. These are our 'prejudices'. The uneducated man who has never heard of the laws of logic may come to quite correct conclusions on such a question, let us say, as the relative chances of drawing a red and a black card by a chance draw from a complete pack, where the facts are simple and the reasoning perfectly straightforward. On the other hand, the learned author of a textbook on logic may be quite unable to come to correct conclusions on a question in which his own interests are deeply involved—such a question, for example, as the economic justification of a kind of taxation which bears specially hardly on himself.

Education does not in itself save us from this disability. It ought to help us in the direction of freedom from prejudice, but it does not necessarily do so. Learned men are often as bound by their prejudices as anyone else. The learned man may defend his most unreasonable prejudices by arguments in correct logical form while the uneducated man defends his by illogical arguments. The difference is plainly not much to the advantage of the learned man. The fact that he can marshal formally correct arguments in defence of his errors may make these more watertight against opposing arguments and against opposing experience. His mastery of the art of thought may simply make his unreasonable opinions more unassailable.

Of course, you, being free from his prejudices, may see the flaw in his reasons for holding the opinions, but this flaw may very well not be in the form of his arguments. It may lie in what he assumes, or in what facts he selects of all possible facts to consider. I do not wish to suggest that correct thinking on correct facts can lead to error, but only that there are other routes to error than lack of logic, and the most logical mind guided by its prejudices can and will find its way to error by one of these other routes.

There was an old opinion (still commonly current) that the lunatic is a person suffering from a defect in his power of reasoning. Now no general statement about lunatics is likely to be true, for the term 'lunacy' covers some dozen mental disorders all with entirely different characters. The kind of lunatic meant by this statement was generally the *paranoiac*, whose main symptom is that he holds some absurd belief, such as that he is the incarnation of some long-dead monarch, or that a group of persons are engaged in a conspiracy against him. In other words, he suffers from *delusions*.

If we actually meet a paranoiac and discuss with him his belief that he is a reincarnation of Napoleon, of Julius Caesar, or of Jesus Christ, we do not find a loss of reasoning power. On the contrary, he reasons most persistently about the very subject of his delusions, and the quality of his reasoning is determined by his intellectual development. If he has a keen, logical intellect he will reason keenly and logically. He will apply the same standard of reasoning in defence of his delusions as he would, if he were sane, apply to the defence of his sane opinions. This standard may be high. It may also be low. Remember that most sane persons have a pretty low standard of reasoning. Ask the average man in the street why he believes that the world is round and he will give you a set of very bad reasons. Ask the flat-earth fanatic why he thinks the world is flat and he will probably give you a much better set, for his reasoning powers have been sharpened in continual controversy with people holding the orthodox view. Yet he is wrong and the illogical man in the street is right. The man with wrong opinions is not necessarily the worse reasoner.

In the same way, the person suffering from insane delusions may show no loss of reasoning power. His defect is that the opinions he holds are very badly wrong, and that his reasoning is used to support these wrong opinions and not to criticise them. Their source is not reasonable. They form a kind of super-prejudice.

When any of us hold the kind of opinions we have called 'prejudices', we have a part of our minds in a condition similar to that of the delusional system of the insane. We too reason to the best of our abilities in defence of our prejudices, but these reasonings are not the real support for our opinions. These are based on other (often quite irrational) grounds.

If we argue directly against the false beliefs of a person suffering from delusional insanity, we shall find our arguments unable to shake his beliefs, because they are not directed against the real cause of those beliefs. The more successful of our arguments will, however, have a result dangerous to ourselves, for they may produce an explosion of violent anger. The deep-seated system of emotions protected so carefully by the set of false beliefs will also be protected by anger and physical violence if the protective system of beliefs is in any way threatened.

The same is true to a lesser degree of the opinions of a sane person grounded on emotional or practical needs. He will not willingly allow those beliefs so necessary to his mental comfort to be overthrown, and if our arguments begin to threaten them he will grow angry or at least peevish. When he begins to show anger instead of reasonable opposition to our arguments, we may press home our advantage, for this is an indication that his beliefs are beginning to be threatened by our arguments.

This use of an opponent's sign of anger as an indication that we have touched what he feels to be a weak spot in his argument is, of course, a perfectly legitimate device in argument. There is also a dishonest trick which may be used in connection with the anger of an opponent. This is the trick of deliberately angering him in order that we may take advantage of the fact that he will argue less efficiently in a condition of anger. This we may do, not only by pressing on a weak point in his argument, but also by adopting a deliberately offensive or insolent manner, by making fun of matters on which he obviously feels strongly, or by the use of such irritating tricks as diversion by irrelevant objection.

Knowledge of the nature of this trick and of its purpose makes the remedy obvious. We must always be determined that nothing shall make us angry in discussion, because, however annoying our opponent may be, we shall best defeat him by keeping our temper under control. If we feel anger arising, this should be a signal to be increasingly courteous to our opponent and increasingly critical of our own position. We can use the first stirrings of anger to detect the weakness of our own position as well as can our opponent.

We must examine a little more closely the psychological nature of these things we have called prejudices. To some objects pleasurable emotions are attached, and we desire these objects and tend to believe any proposition whose truth would secure them. To other objects, unpleasurable emotions are attached, and we turn from these objects and tend to believe any proposition which denies their reality. More simply we may say that we tend to believe what we desire or need to be true and to disbelieve what we desire or need to be false. If we have put our last sovereign on a horse running at a hundred to one, we fervently believe that he will win and we shall hotly contest a friend's proposition that he cannot run and will most likely come in last. Similarly, if a man is suffering from a dangerous illness he tends to refuse to believe

16

that his illness can really be fatal because his desire for life makes him unwilling to accept the evidence that he is unlikely to recover.

Sometimes it is obvious how the emotions which determine our acceptance of some propositions and rejection of others came into existence. Practically all men desire money and comfort, and fear ruin and death, so they will tend to accept propositions whose truth would secure their wealth, comfort, and security of living, and reject those whose truth would threaten them. We can see how general this law is when we notice how nearly universal is the rule that those who have possessions (even a few) are politically on the side of preservation of the existing order, while revolutionaries are, on the whole, recruited from the non-possessors.

Sometimes however, the connection between emotions and prejudices is more obscure. The emotions lying behind a prejudice may be a relic of the emotional life of early childhood. Our childish love for our father or our resentment against his discipline may be the determining cause of our adult reverence for authority or of our rebellion against it. Which of these two factors was the stronger in our childhood may thus determine whether we shall be monarchists or republicans, conservatives or revolutionaries. Similarly, our sympathy with oppressed peoples may be based on our childhood's phantasies of rescuing our mother from distress.

Whether the connection between the prejudice and the emotion giving rise to it seems obvious, as in the case of political opinions determined by the amount of a man's possessions, or obscure, as in the case of opinions determined by his childhood relationship to his father, recognition of this connection is not possible for the holder of the prejudice. It is the essential nature of a prejudice that the connection should not be apparent. The prejudiced person believes that he holds his opinion on entirely rational grounds. If he understood that his opinion was really based on irrational grounds, his prejudice would disappear. He might still hold his former opinion or he might reject it, but if he held it it would have to be on other grounds than those on which it was based when it was a prejudice. The strength of the prejudice depends on the fact that he cannot become aware of these irrational grounds on which it is based. The further these grounds are hidden from his awareness, the more strongly is the prejudice held.

1915 words

In your notebook, write down the time taken to read this passage.

Now, before you do anything else, turn over and answer the Tests.

COMPREHENSION TESTS

A. Retention

Do not refer back to the passage

1 What was the old opinion (still commonly current) about the lunatic?
2 What does the writer say is the main symptom shown by the paranoiac?
3 When we argue with someone and he begins to show anger instead of reasonable opposition to our arguments, what does this indicate?
4 What is the dishonest trick which may be used in connection with the anger of an opponent?
5 If, in discussion, we feel anger rising, what does this indicate we should do?
6 Why, in the writer's opinion, if a man is suffering from a dangerous illness, does he tend to refuse to believe that his illness can really be fatal?
7 On which side, politically, do those who have possessions (even a few) tend to be?
8 What may be the determining cause of our adult reverence for authority or of our rebellion against it?
9 On what grounds does the prejudiced person believe that he holds his opinion?
10 On what does the strength of a prejudice depend?

B. Understanding and Interpretation

Do not refer back to the passage

Comments on probable answers are given in the appropriate section of the answer key at the back of the book.

1 List the main points made in the passage.
2 What can be deduced from the passage concerning the most effective ways of combating prejudice in our opinions?
3 What do you infer are the dangers of being prejudiced in one's thinking?
4 What do you think is the writer's estimation of the value of education in enabling individuals to think clearly and logically?
5 Explain the following *in your own words*: prejudice; delusions; fanatic; proposition; the existing order.

C. Discussion and Evaluation

You may refer to the passage

1 What do *you* think is the value of education in enabling individuals to think clearly?
2 What are your own prejudices?
3 Should we try to think clearly and logically at all times or are there matters about which it doesn't matter if we are prejudiced?
4 Select an issue on which you have very strong opinions and attempt a fair and complete statement of the point of view which conflicts with your own.
5 Attempt a critical evaluation of the passage. Give special consideration to the writer's intentions in saying what he does.

Practice Work

During the next week, as you read your daily newspaper and any other light and fairly easy reading matter, continue trying to read faster *and more critically*. Ask yourself questions like these:

1 What is the writer telling me?
2 Are his facts correct?
3 What is his authority for saying this?
4 What is he trying to achieve by saying it?
5 Am I being convinced by logical reasoning or by emotion? Or prejudice?
6 How has the writer presented his information?
7 Does good presentation hide a weak case?
8 Has the style of writing influenced me in my acceptance or rejection of what he says?
9 What is my final judgement (in the light of answers to the above questions)?
10 If the writer fails to communicate and/or convince, how, why and in which parts particularly does he fail?

Passage Three

As you read the following passage, continue trying to read faster and to retain and understand the material better.

PASSAGE THREE

from *The True Believer* by Eric Hoffer

When the moment is ripe, only the fanatic can hatch a genuine mass movement. Without him the disaffection engendered by militant men of words remains undirected and can vent itself only in pointless and easily suppressed disorders. Without him the initiated reforms, even when drastic, leave the old way of life unchanged, and any change in government usually amounts to no more than a transfer of power from one set of men of action to another. Without him there can perhaps be no new beginning.

When the old order begins to fall apart, many of the vociferous men of words, who prayed so long for the day, are in a funk. The first glimpse of the face of anarchy frightens them out of their wits. They forget all they said about the 'poor simple folk' and run for help to strong men of action—princes, generals, administrators, bankers, landowners—who know how to deal with the rabble and how to stem the tide of chaos.

Not so the fanatic. Chaos is his element. When the old order begins to crack, he wades in with all his might and recklessness to blow the whole hated present to high heaven. He glories in the sight of a world coming to a sudden end. To hell with reforms! All that already exists is rubbish, and there is no sense in reforming rubbish. He justifies his will to anarchy with the plausible assertion that there can be no new beginning so long as the old clutters the landscape. He shoves aside the frightened men of words, if they are still around, though he continues to extol their doctrines and mouth their slogans. He alone knows the innermost craving of the masses in action: the craving for communion, for the mustering of the host, for the dissolution of cursed individuality in the majesty and grandeur of a mighty whole. Posterity is king; and woe to those, inside and outside the movement, who hug and hang on to the present.

Whence come the fanatics? Mostly from the ranks of the non-creative men of words. The most significant division between men of words is between those who can find fulfilment in creative work and those who cannot. The creative man of words, no matter how bitterly he may criticise and deride the existing order, is actually attached to the present. His passion is to reform and not to destroy. When the mass movement remains wholly in his keeping, he turns it into a mild affair. The reforms he initiates are of the surface, and life flows on without a sudden break. But such a development is possible only when the anarchic action of the masses does not come into play, either because the old order abdicates without a struggle or because the man of words allies himself with strong men of action the moment chaos threatens to break loose. When the struggle with the old order is bitter and chaotic and victory can be won only by utmost unity and self-sacrifice, the creative man of words is usually shoved aside and the management of affairs falls into the hands of the non-creative men of words—the eternal misfits and the fanatical contemners of the present.

The man who wants to write a great book, paint a great picture, create an architectural masterpiece, become a great scientist, and knows that never in all eternity will he be able to realise this, his innermost desire, can find no peace in a stable order—old or new. He sees his life as irrevocably spoiled and the world perpetually out of joint. He feels at home only in a state of chaos. Even when he submits to or imposes an iron discipline, he is but submitting to or shaping the indispensable instrument for attaining a state of eternal flux, eternal becoming. Only when engaged in change does he have a sense of freedom and the feeling that he is growing and developing. It is because he can never be reconciled with his self that he fears finality and a fixed order of things. Marat, Robespierre, Lenin, Mussolini and Hitler are outstanding examples of fanatics arising from the ranks of non-creative men of words. Peter Viereck points out that most of the Nazi bigwigs had artistic and literary ambitions which they could not realise. Hitler tried painting and architecture; Goebbels, drama, the novel and poetry; Rosenberg, architecture and philosophy; von Shirach, poetry; Funk, music; Streicher, painting. 'Almost all were failures, not only by the usual vulgar criterion of success but by their own artistic criteria.' Their artistic and literary ambitions 'were originally far deeper than political ambitions: and were integral parts of their personalities'.

The creative man of words is ill at ease in the atmosphere of an active movement. He feels that its whirl and passion sap his creative energies. So long as he is conscious of the creative flow within him, he will not find fulfilment in leading millions and in winning victories. The result is that, once the movement starts rolling, he either retires voluntarily or is pushed aside. Moreover, since the genuine man of words can never wholeheartedly and for

21

long suppress his critical faculty, he is inevitably cast in the role of the heretic. Thus unless the creative man of words stifles the newborn movement by allying himself with practical men of action or unless he dies at the right moment, he is likely to end up either a shunned recluse or in exile or facing a firing squad.

The danger of the fanatic to the development of a movement is that he cannot settle down. Once victory has been won and the new order begins to crystallise, the fanatic becomes an element of strain and disruption. The taste for strong feeling drives him on to search for mysteries yet to be revealed and secret doors yet to be opened. He keeps groping for extremes. Thus on the morrow of victory most mass movements find themselves in the grip of dissension. The ardour which yesterday found an outlet in a life-and-death struggle with external enemies now vents itself in violent disputes and clash of factions. Hatred has become a habit. With no more outside enemies to destroy, the fanatics make enemies of one another. Hitler—himself a fanatic—could diagnose with precision the state of mind of the fanatics who plotted against him within the ranks of the National Socialist party. In his order to the newly appointed chief of the SA after the purge of Röhm in 1934 he speaks of those who will not settle down: '. . . without realising it, [they] have found in nihilism their ultimate confession of faith . . . their unrest and disquietude can find satisfaction only in some conspiratorial activity of the mind, in perpetually plotting the disintegration of whatever the set-up of the moment happens to be.' As was often the case with Hitler, his accusations against antagonists (inside and outside the Reich) were a self-revelation. He, too, particularly in his last days, found in nihilism his 'ultimate philosophy and valediction'.

If allowed to have their way, the fanatics may split a movement into schism and heresies which threaten its existence. Even when the fanatics do not breed dissension, they can still wreck the movement by driving it to attempt the impossible. Only the entrance of a practical man of action can save the achievements of the movement.

1310 words

Write down the time taken to read this passage and then turn over and answer the Tests.

COMPREHENSION TESTS

A. Retention

Do not refer back to the passage

1 With what assertion does the fanatic justify his will to anarchy?
2 What does the writer say is 'the innermost craving of the masses in action'?
3 From whose ranks does the writer say fanatics come?
4 What is the most significant division between men of words?
5 Name two of the characteristics, given by the writer, of the fanatic.
6 The writer tells us that 'most of the Nazi bigwigs had artistic and literary ambitions that they could not realise'. What was Funk's unrealized ambition?
7 Why, in the writer's opinion, does the creative man of words feel ill at ease in the atmosphere of an active movement?
8 What is the danger of a fanatic to the development of a movement?
9 What happens when fanatics have no more outside enemies to destroy?
10 What does the writer say is the only thing that can save a movement from the destructive influence of fanatics?

B. Understanding and Interpretation

Do not refer back to the passage

1 What do you feel is the writer's attitude towards fanatics?
2 What are the main differences between the creative and the non-creative men of words?
3 Why does the writer feel that, once victory has been won and the new order begins to crystallize, the fanatic is a danger to a movement?
4 From what the writer says, do you feel that, had he been successful in the Second World War, Hitler would have established a stable order of society, 'a Reich that would last for a thousand years'?
5 Which of the five fanatics the writer lists, if any, do not appear to fit the pattern of fanaticism he describes? Give reasons for your opinion.

C. Discussion and Evaluation

You may refer back to the passage

1 How does the writer define a fanatic? How far do you agree with his definition?
2 How sound are the writer's arguments?
3 What has been the role of the fanatic and of extremist movements in twentieth-century British politics? What information can be obtained from the passage to suggest reasons for the apparent ineffectiveness of British fanatics?
4 Discuss the writer's style. What effect has this had on your acceptance or rejection of the points he makes?
5 What are your own opinions of the value or otherwise of fanatics in (*a*) political and (*b*) religious movements?

Practice Work

During the next week, continue trying to read faster and more critically. Each day select a passage from your daily newspaper or a similar source, calculate how many words it contains (count the number of words in a ten-line section near the end, divide by ten to obtain the average number of words per line, then multiply by the number of lines in the passage—choose an article that is about 500–1000 words in length), read the passage and write down the time taken. To test comprehension, when you have finished reading make a list of the *main* points and/or the *important* facts it contained. Check your answers by reference back to the passage. If there is someone who will check your answers independently, this would be preferable.

Passage Four

As you read the following passage continue trying to read faster and to retain and understand the material better.

PASSAGE FOUR

from *Six Days or Forever?* by Ray Ginger

Sitting on hard wooden benches under the maple trees, spectators; sitting cross-legged in the grass, spectators; pressing close around the wooden platform where Judge Raulston sat at an informal table, where Bryan sat in the witness stand, where Darrow negligently rested one hand on a table, his right foot on a chair, and toyed with his gold-rimmed spectacles, spectators; perched in the branches of the trees, small boys absorbed by the spectacle—they all watched while Darrow plucked the protective feathers from William Jennings Bryan, and twisted the head off his prestige, and flung him flopping to his onetime admirers.

Darrow began quietly, asking if Bryan had not 'given considerable study to the Bible'. Bryan admitted it. Then Darrow began his ruthless efforts to make Bryan admit that the Bible could not always be taken literally, that it was sometimes vague, that the Butler Act was fatally indefinite when it forbade the teachings of 'any theory that denies the story of the Divine Creation of man as taught in the Bible'.

Did Bryan think that Jonah had remained three days in a whale's belly?

Bryan replied: 'I believe in a God who can make a whale and can make a man and make both do what he pleases.'

Was this whale just an ordinary big fish, or had God created him especially for this purpose?

The Bible does not say, said Bryan; therefore I do not know.

'But', Darrow persisted, 'do you believe He made them—that He made such a fish and that it was big enough to swallow Jonah?'

'Yes, sir,' said Bryan stoutly. 'Let me add: One miracle is just as easy to believe as another.'

'It is for me,' said Darrow caustically.

And Bryan, stinging already, hotly replied in Darrow's exact words. Darrow began asking whether Joshua had really made the sun stand still. Did the sun go around the earth, as the Bible implied?

Attorney-General Stewart, who had worked so hard to limit the trial to narrow factual issues, now strove to maintain that barrier. He objected to any further questioning of Bryan, and he asked that the prior questions be stricken from the record.

But Judge Raulston was enjoying himself. He said: 'I will hear Mr. Bryan.'

Darrow's febricant questions began again. Is there any conceivable way that a day could be lengthened unless the earth stood still? What would happen to the earth if it suddenly stopped? Wouldn't it become a molten mass?

Bryan was increasingly ruffled. His palm-leaf fan, which had formerly beat vigorously, now paused, flickered, scratched in nervous ineffectuality. He flushed at some questions, fleered at Darrow because of others.

Darrow had never faced a more difficult witness: he could seldom get Bryan to answer any question directly. Bryan backpedalled and parried; Darrow continued to probe. The Tennessee sun ate into them, and Darrow's efforts brought sweat through his shirt, and he tugged repeatedly at his suspenders and twirled his glasses in his hand and despised Bryan's tight hard smile.

Doubtless Darrow's original intent in getting Bryan onto the witness stand had been mixed: the legal shrewdness of forcing a leader of the prosecution to admit that the Bible must be interpreted, the glee to be found in exposing a fanatic, the exquisite pleasure that any craftsman finds in using his tools. But in the heat of the deed all of these motives coalesced into a dominant emotion: anger.

Bryan testified for an hour and a half. Throughout that time he tried to evade. The more he did so, the more angry Darrow became. During the trial he had found repeated frustration. Judge Raulston had stopped him from examining the scientific witnesses, and had repeatedly ruled against him on points large and small. This had led to Darrow's outburst at Raulston—a double-edged episode: Darrow's success at gulling his oppressor may have mitigated but could not erase his coerced apology. Now Bryan was trying to escape, and Darrow's pent-up resentment drove him in pursuit. Relentlessly, viciously, he brought Bryan to bay.

When, asked Darrow, did the flood occur? Bryan would 'not attempt to fix the date'.

But didn't every printed Bible say that the flood had happened about 4004 B.C.?

Yes, that was the estimate given.

How was the estimate arrived at?

Bryan: 'I never made a calculation.'

Darrow: 'A calculation from what?'

Bryan: 'I could not say.'

Darrow: 'From the generations of man?'
Bryan: 'I would not want to say that.'
Darrow: 'What do you think?'
Bryan: 'I do not think about things I don't think about.'
Darrow: 'Do you think about things you do think about?'
Bryan: 'Well, sometimes.'

The laughter, with Judge Raulston an eager participant, marked the end of the conflict, the beginning of rout.

Again Stewart, joined now by McKenzie, tried to rescue him. But Bryan was grievously hurt, and he would not be rescued. Turning to the audience, he indicated the defense lawyers: 'These gentlemen have not had much chance—they did not come here to try this case. They came to try revealed religion. I am here to defend it, and they can ask me any question they please.'

There was loud clapping.

Darrow said: 'Great applause from the bleachers.'
Bryan: 'From those whom you call "yokels".'
Darrow: 'I have never called them "yokels".'

They wrangled on. Bryan said: 'Those are the people whom you insult.'

Darrow: 'You insult every man of science and learning in the world because he does not believe in your fool religion.'

Now Judge Raulston protested: 'I will not stand for that.'

Darrow: 'For what he is doing?'

The effrontery of it startled the judge into saying: 'I am talking to both of you.'

Again Stewart tried to halt the questioning (a Southern reporter called his efforts 'pathetic'). Again Raulston said: 'To stop it now would not be just to Mr. Bryan. He wants to ask the other gentleman questions along the same lines.'

Darrow kept worrying at the witness about the dates that Bishop Ussher, calculating from the ages of the various prophets, had assigned to Scriptural episodes. The Bishop had computed the date of Creation as 4004 B.C. He had been even more specific: this happy event had occurred on 23 October at 9 a.m.

A voice in the audience added: 'Eastern Standard Time.'

Bryan wriggled and writhed, but Darrow kept pressing him. And eventually Bryan gave answers.

Did Bryan believe that all of the species on the earth had come into being in the 4,200 years, by the Bishop's dating, since the Flood occurred? Yes, said Bryan finally, he did believe it.

Didn't Bryan know that many civilizations had existed for more

28

than 5,000 years? Said Bryan: 'I have never felt a great deal of interest in the effort that has been made to dispute the Bible by the speculations of men, or the investigations of men.'

Didn't Bryan know that many old religions described a Flood? No, he had 'never felt it necessary to look up some competing religions'.

Had Bryan ever read Tylor's *Primitive Culture*, or Boas? Had he ever tried to find out about the other peoples of the earth and how old their civilizations are? Said Bryan: 'No, sir, I have been so well satisfied with the Christian religion that I have spent no time trying to find arguments against it.'

He went further yet: 'I have all the information I want to live by and to die by.'

Darrow: 'And that's all you are interested in?'

Bryan: 'I am not looking for any more on religion.'

Now Bryan, condoned by Raulston, began a series of discursive speeches about other religions. It was mainly hearsay: what he had been told by some anonymous man in Rangoon, what he had learned about Buddhism from an Englishman converted to that religion, and so on. (Dudley Field Malone surreptitiously bought his wife a bottle of soda pop.)

Did Bryan know how old the earth was? No, he didn't. Wasn't there some scientist that he respected? He named George M. Price and 'a man named Wright, who taught at Oberlin.' Darrow called them mountebanks.

By this time Bryan's self-esteem was suppurating, and his wits entirely deserted him. Having discredited himself with everybody who did not believe in the literal truth of the Bible, he now destroyed himself with those who did. It took one deft question by Darrow, and a six-word reply.

Darrow asked: 'Do you think the earth was made in six days?'

Bryan: 'Not six days of twenty-four hours.'

(Sitting under a tree at the fringes of the crowd, surrounded by fundamentalists, Kirtley Mather heard the startled gasps. His neighbors were aghast. 'What does he want to say that for?' they demanded of each other.)

Stewart again tried to stop it. 'What,' he asked, 'is the purpose of this examination?'

Not even waiting for the judge to answer, Bryan said that the defense lawyers had 'no other purpose than ridiculing every Christian who believes in the Bible.'

Darrow said directly to Bryan: 'We have the purpose of pre-

29

venting bigots and ignoramuses from controlling the education of the United States and you know it—and that is all.'

Dudley Malone observed that Bryan seemed to be trying to get into the trial record some evidence to disprove the scientists' statements.

A porcine-eyed Bryan leaped to his feet and shouted to the crowd in the courtyard: 'I am not trying to get anything into the record. I am simply trying to protect the word of God against the greatest atheist or agnostic in the United States!'

The applause was thunderous and prolonged. When it died down, Darrow said: 'I wish I could get a picture of these clackers.'

And again Stewart protested against any continuance of the examination. They argued and argued. Judge Raulston said that of course the questions would not be proper testimony before a jury, but that he was permitting them for the purposes of the record on the appeal.

Not so, said Bryan, he was not talking for the benefit of any appellate court. He was talking for only one reason: 'I want the Christian world to know that any atheist, agnostic, unbeliever, can question me any time as to my belief in God, and I will answer him.' They argued and argued, and the questions went on.

Darrow read the passage from Genesis: 'The morning and the evening were the first day.' He asked if Bryan also believed that the sun was created on the fourth day. Yes, Bryan did. Darrow asked how there could have been a morning and evening without any sun. Bryan had no answer.

Those 'days' in Genesis, Darrow asked, they might have been long periods? Yes, said Bryan, the Creation might have lasted for 'millions of years'. He squirmed vigorously. He did not want to commit himself, and Darrow forced the choice upon him. So far as the 'days' are concerned, said Bryan, 'My impression is that they were periods, but I would not attempt to argue against anybody who wanted to believe in literal days.'

Darrow began to ask about Eve and the serpent. The Bible said that God had punished the serpent for having tempted Eve.

Darrow asked: 'Do you think that is why the serpent is compelled to crawl upon its belly?'

Bryan: 'I believe that.'

Darrow: 'Have you any idea how the snake went before that time?'

Bryan: 'No, sir.'

Darrow: 'Do you know whether he walked on his tail or not?'

Bryan: 'No, sir I have no way to know.'

They laughed. The crowd laughed. Now Bryan's nervous condition was eloquent. His hands trembled, his lips were quivering, his face was suffused and dark. He broke completely. He said:

'Your Honor, I think I can shorten this testimony.' He would answer the question. Yes, he would. And he jumped to his feet and turned to the people with outstretched hands and he shouted at an almost hysterical pitch:

'I want the world to know that this man, who does not believe in a God, is trying to use a court in Tennessee—'

Darrow: 'I object to that.'

Bryan: '—to slur at it—'

Darrow: 'I object to your statement. I am examining you on your fool ideas that no intelligent Christian on earth believes.'

And the judge adjourned court for the day.

Darrow's admirers swarmed around him, laughing and shaking his hand.

Bryan stood almost alone, deserted, a tired expression on his sagging face. It had been a long afternoon, and the twilight was closing in.

(Kirtley Mather heard the fundamentalists around him planning a group visit to Bryan that night to tell him, to his face, how much they disapproved of the concessions he had made. 'I do not think they were twenty-four-hour days.' The Judas.)

Indeed a long day: the judge's citation of Darrow for contempt, and reading of the scientific statements by Hays, Darrow's mock apology, more scientific statements, the examination of Bryan. A day of reversals: at noontime, Darrow vulnerable and Bryan vicariously regal; four hours later, Darrow ascendant and Bryan a maunderer.

'The words of a wise man's mouth are gracious, but the lips of a fool will swallow up himself. The beginning of the words of his mouth is foolishness; and the end of his talk is mischievous madness' (Ecclesiastes x: 12–13).

2180 words

Write down the time taken to read this passage and then turn over and answer the Tests.

COMPREHENSION TESTS

A. Retention

Do not refer back to the passage

1 Give the names of both the prosecution counsel and the defence counsel.
2 Which Act forbade the teaching of 'any theory that denies the story of the Divine Creation of man as taught in the Bible'?
3 Did Bryan think that Jonah had remained three days in a whale's belly?
4 Give one of the reasons, stated by the writer, for Darrow's getting Bryan on to the witness stand.
5 At what date had Bishop Ussher computed the Creation?
6 By what means had Bryan obtained his information about other religions?
7 What was Bryan's reply to Darrow's question: 'Do you think the earth was made in six days?'
8 What was the term used by the writer to describe those who believed in the literal truth of the Bible?
9 How long did Bryan concede the Creation might have lasted for?
10 How does the writer describe this particular day in the hearing?

B. Understanding and Interpretation

Do not refer back to the passage

1 Which statement marks the turning point in Darrow's cross-examination of Bryan?
2 Why had Darrow 'never faced a more difficult witness' than Bryan?
3 What was Darrow trying to prove in his cross-examination of Bryan?
4 Why did Darrow begin his questioning by asking if Bryan had not 'given considerable study to the Bible'?
5 Explain the following *in your own words*: suspenders; mitigated; discursive; porcine-eyed; citation.

C. Discussion and Evaluation

You may refer back to the passage

1 Was Bryan a fanatic?
2 What evidence, if any, is there in this passage to suggest a conflict between science and religion?

3 The Butler Act sought to put a limitation on what could be taught in Tennessean schools. Should such limitations exist? What limitations exist in Britain?

4 Darrow appeared to win this particular battle against the fundamentalists. What do you feel would be the jury's verdict at this trial? Why? (Find out afterwards what the jury's verdict was.)

5 Attempt an evaluation of the arguments of both the prosecution and the defence, as revealed by this extract.

Practice Work

Continue the practice work recommended at the end of Passage Three.

Passage Five

As you read the following passage, continue trying to read faster and to retain and understand the material better.

PASSAGE FIVE

Not So Simple as ABC, by G. R. Wainwright

Within the English educational system, the only instruction in reading most people ever receive is in the first years of the junior school. That is, we are taught how to read, and then it is largely assumed that our work in English lessons is sufficient to make us efficient in our reading habits by the time we leave school and begin work. It rather gives the impression that English readers are satisfied with their ability to use this particular communication skill. Yet this is not so. Many business men and industrial executives, particularly, find their daily routine reading of correspondence, reports, newspapers and journals a chore, and in some cases a problem of some seriousness because they simply cannot read quickly enough. To solve this problem, many firms and some further education establishments are now running courses in efficient reading, designed to help anyone to increase his reading speed without suffering loss in comprehension.

The origin of these courses lies in the United States, where the slowness of the average reader and his low level of comprehension caused concern among educationists in the twenties. As a result of research, reading-improvement courses in schools and colleges began to appear in the thirties. During the war, courses were provided for Service personnel. After the war, with the increasingly urgent problem of improving managers' and workers' use of communication skills to enable them to meet more effectively the demands made upon them, courses in reading efficiency became available in most large industrial and business organisations. Reading 'clinics' were established, in which further research was undertaken and which contributed to the increasing effectiveness of these courses.

In Britain, reading efficiency courses first became popular in the mid-fifties. In the last ten years many British firms have introduced courses for their own employees and a number of colleges have become interested. For the would-be efficient British reader there is now a variety of self-instruction books and courses from which he can choose. As the demand increases, so do the opportunities.

All these courses are basically similar in their aims and in what they teach. The methods used, however, vary considerably. Some courses use specially designed films and mechanical devices in association with teaching by an instructor. Others merely use reading exercises combined with instruction in the skills to be learned. At the moment, there is no evidence that courses which use films and other aids are any more successful than those which do not. My own experience is that, for many readers, the films at present available are more of a hindrance than a help. How successful students are, who work on their own with the aid of books, it is difficult to tell, but it seems to be true for most people that they achieve more by being a member of a group under the guidance of an instructor.

The content of these courses is based principally on an analysis of the skills used by 'naturally' efficient readers. We do not know why some people read faster than others—it does not appear to depend on intelligence—but we can find out how these faster, more efficient readers deal with materials. We know that they do not 'regress' (read something twice) habitually, as a slower reader tends to do. They have a wider span of perception. Since the eye 'reads' only when it is momentarily 'fixed' on the materials, the amount of material taken in at each fixation obviously has an effect on the speed at which people read. They do not 'subvocalise' ('hear' the voice of the author as they read silently) all the time. They have a wider vocabulary, greater powers of concentration, a rhythmic reading sweep across the page, and they can anticipate the nature of the material that follows. They have a clear knowledge of their purpose before beginning to read.

Too often the poorer reader simply picks up the material and begins reading without really knowing why (apart from the fact, perhaps, that he has to). The most difficult element to teach in a short course is the efficient reader's generally wider and more thoughtful approach to knowledge and experience. That is why my own 10 or 12 week course operates in conjunction with a complementary general studies course which lasts for a full year.

The courses we ran at the Hull College of Technology attracted people from a wide range of occupations, not just business men and industrialists, but policemen, housewives, postmen, teachers, engineers, civil servants, trainees, and students following many courses. We have even had an application from a 12-year-old grammar school boy. In the last three years, over 250 people have attended the courses and only one man has suffered a reduction in his reading speed. The same man, however, improved his comprehension of the material he read by over 30 per cent. The average results on the courses run in the last year have been extremely satisfying—an increase in reading speed of well over 100 per cent and an improvement in comprehension of over 25 per cent—and individual students have achieved results double those of the average student.

But the figures are only a part of the story. It is the intangible benefits that students report which give the most encouragement —a man who had not previously read a novel for seven years becoming an avid reader and a woman who was able to deal with her daily reading at work in half the time enjoying breakfast in the morning without a feeling of inadequacy. Results like these are the real satisfactions of reading efficiency courses.

The permanence of these achievements is still in doubt. Tests that I conducted at the Hull College of Technology indicate that a year after the end of the course many students have fallen back to a reading speed midway between the speed with which they started the course and the one they attained by the end. Still, for most people an appreciable gain. The reason for this falling off in speed is probably a failure to continue regular practice after attending the short course. After all, even for teenagers we are trying to change habits of several years' duration. The short course merely enables students to begin the process of change and, regrettably, too many of them expect, overnight, permanent improvements—'instant' rapid reading.

The case for efficient reading has been well proved in the last 20 years. Anyone who feels that his reading speed or his level of comprehension is lower than it should be, or who needs to improve his efficiency in order to cope more effectively with the demands of his job, can be recommended with confidence to buy one of the several self-instruction books available or, better still, to join the nearest available industrial or college course in efficient reading.

1040 words

Write down the time taken to read this passage and then turn over and answer the Tests.

COMPREHENSION TESTS

A. Retention

Do not refer back to the passage

1 What reason does the writer give for many businessmen and industrial executives finding reading 'a chore and in some cases a problem of some seriousness'?
2 Where did reading efficiency courses originate?
3 When did reading efficiency courses first become popular in Britain?
4 What evidence is there that courses which use films and other aids are more successful than those which do not?
5 On what are reading efficiency courses principally based?
6 What is the most difficult element of reading efficiency to teach in a short course?
7 What were the average results obtained on the writer's courses over the previous years?
8 The writer states that 'it is the intangible benefits that students report which give the most encouragement'. Give one of the examples quoted by the writer in support of this statement.
9 How much of the improvement made can students expect to retain?
10 What is the reason the writer gives for the need to continue regular practice after attending a course in reading efficiency?

B. Understanding and Interpretation

Do not refer back to the passage

1 *In your own words*, describe how the eyes move when reading.
2 What are the main differences between poor readers and efficient readers? Write down your answer in table form, e.g.:

Poor Readers	Efficient Readers
(1)	
(2)	
(3)	
(4), etc.	

3 Does reading faster generally mean a lowering of the level of comprehension? Give reasons for your answer, which should be based only on the information given in the passage.
4 Why do you think it is the intangible benefits which students report which give the most encouragement to a tutor?
5 Explain the following *in your own words*: efficient; comprehension; an avid reader; subvocalize; 'instant' rapid reading.

C. Discussion and Evaluation

You may refer back to the passage

1 Why is there a need for reading efficiency courses for adults?
2 How efficient a reader are you? Do you feel you can improve your efficiency?
3 How far do you agree or disagree with the points the writer makes? How far has your answer to this question been affected by your answer to question C1?
4 What do you feel are the 'intangible benefits' of becoming a more efficient reader?
5 How important is the more efficient use of language communication skills (reading, writing, listening, and speaking) in modern business and industry and in what ways?

Practice Work

Continue the practice recommended at the end of Passage Three, but from now on *skim* everything you read before actually reading it. Allow yourself approximately *one minute per 1000 words*. As you skim through the material try to see the way in which the writer has organized the points he is making or the information he is giving. Try also to pick out the main points, the important facts and those parts of the material which, because of their novelty or their complexity, are going to prove rather more difficult to understand. You will find that skimming or pre-reading material in this way will help you to define more closely your purpose in reading it, will give you a clearer idea of what to expect from the material and will generally tell you *how* to read the material. In some cases you will find that skimming alone is sufficient, in others, you will realize the material has to be read slowly and carefully for full and accurate comprehension. But remember that slow reading now would have been fast reading only a few weeks ago.

Include the time spent in skimming or pre-reading in the total time taken to read each passage.

Passage Six

As you read the following passage, continue trying to read faster and to retain and understand the material better.

39

PASSAGE SIX

from *How to Study* by Harry Maddox

A System of Study: SQ3R

An aid to systematic study which has proved of value in American Colleges and Universities is the system called SQ3R. The SQ3R stands for:

Survey   Question   Read   Recite   Revise

(1) *Survey*. In brief, this means that instead of picking up a textbook and reading one of its chapters over and over, you should first survey: that is find out all you can about the aims and purpose of the book, read the author's preface, study the table of contents and the index, read the chapter summaries (if there are summaries) and skim your way rapidly through the book. Keep in mind your own purpose in study, the syllabus you are trying to cover, and the relevance of the book to your own special interests. And if the book does not suit your purpose, if it is not well written, and at the right level of difficulty, search around until you find a better one. In other words, make a reconnaissance before you start your main work, and get an over-all perspective of what lies before you.

(2) *Question*. The second preparatory step—asking questions—is also important. This entails going rapidly through the chapters of the book which you are going to tackle, and jotting down such questions as occur to you. This is useful because it motivates you and gives you a purpose: it forces you to think and to marshal such knowledge as you already have. Many good authors help the reader by clearly stating a problem in their introductory sentences or specifically confronting the reader with questions. And if you persist in maintaining a questioning attitude, you will in time come to read books critically, you will ask what evidence the author has for his statements and whether what he is saying is consistent with what you already know or believe. No intelligent person merely reads a book. He cannot help dwelling on particular points as he reads, and contrasting or uniting them with other points that he has just grasped.

(3) *Reading*. Next comes reading proper. The first reading of a textbook chapter usually needs to be rather slow and thorough. If you are a voracious reader of novels or detective stories you must

not carry over to textbooks your habit of rapid reading for entertainment. Most good textbook chapters have a structure of headings and sub-headings which you need to keep in the back of your mind as you read. Often you must turn back to previous pages to remind yourself of some fact or argument. If the subject is illustrated by graphs or by diagrams, you will often be well advised to copy them out or elaborate them. Complex arguments and masses of information can often be presented briefly and neatly in a table or graph. Hence, if you are foolish enough to skip the graphs or tables you will often miss the major points that the author is trying to make. Moreover, most people will find, if they will take the trouble to master them, that graphs and diagrams are much more easily remembered than long verbal statements, and serve as convenient foundations around which to build a structure of knowledge.

(4) *Recitation.* A single reading is never enough, even though you read actively with intent to remember. The next stage in study is therefore recitation. Bacon said: 'If you read anything over twenty times you will not learn it by heart so easily as if you were to read it only ten, trying to repeat it between whiles, and when memory failed looking at the book.'

Recitation is certainly an old-fashioned method, and to many it suggests classes in the infant school, learning off, parrot-fashion, the multiplication table or a verse by Sir Walter Scott. The last thing we want is that our learning should be rote and meaningless.

By recitation is meant here not word for word repetition, or learning by heart, but outlining the substance of a passage. The outline provides the framework into which more details can be fitted in subsequent recitation.

Literal word-for-word recitation is only applicable when formulae or foreign language vocabularies or anatomical facts have to be memorized, and, on such materials, it is of advantage to use about three-quarters of the available time in recitation. But nothing should ever be learnt as an isolated, meaningless unit. Formulae can be derived from first principles, foreign language words can be understood by studying their roots and derivations, and anatomical facts can be memorized better by starting with simplified diagrams to which detail is added. Sometimes, however, things have to be taken as given and they have to be committed to memory. Then recitation is of great help. With more meaningful material, recitation must not degenerate into rote learning and become a substitute for thought; and it may be of little use in the early stages of learning.

So recitation is of most value in learning those things which have to be got off by heart, such as the multiplication table and the alphabet; but it is still good practice, after reading each major section of a chapter, to lay the book on one side and try and recall what you have been reading. This simple procedure is often revealing. Sometimes you can recall very little and must conclude that your learning is in a very immature stage. More frequently you will realize that there are some specific gaps in your knowledge which you must go back and fill in. Certainly the procedure cures that habit, often a relic of school days, of thinking that because you have read through a chapter, you have 'done it' and know it. In my experience, four or five readings and recitations are usually required before textbook materials of average difficulty can be mastered. Repetition of itself is of no value, but each repetition, if you are reading actively and alertly, should add to your insight into the material.

(5) *Revision*. The final step of SQ3R is Revision. Revision should not be regarded as something to be undertaken just before examinations. One of the most practical results of memory experiments is that material that has to be retained over long periods should be studied and re-studied. Memories become stronger and stronger with each re-learning, and forgetting proceeds more slowly. Let us examine the curve of forgetting. Material into which there is real insight is not forgotten. For all other materials forgetting is at first very rapid and then becomes slower.

The permanence of your learning should be of concern to you. Ask yourself how much you can remember of your school Latin or Geometry or French, and you will probably find that unless you have been recently using or practising a subject, the greater part of it will have been forgotten. American studies suggest that typically, after two years, the average student scores only about 30 per cent. of the perfect score on a test of factual knowledge. General principles and general understandings, on the other hand, are retained for much longer.

Common experience suggests that the details of what we learn fade very quickly, often within the first hour or so. Indeed, in listening to an hour's lecture much of the early part of the lecture may have been forgotten well before the end—so that experienced teachers repeat and recapitulate the important points of their lectures at the end. To prevent the sudden and catastrophic loss which takes place so early, early revision is required. That means going over the lecture or piece of work again as soon as possible afterwards, thinking about it, or discussing it with others or applying the facts and knowledge in some practical exercises. You should certainly go over your notes of lectures, work periods and experiments the very same day—even if it is only for a few minutes.

This practical advice is seldom carried out, I fancy, because, having taken down some written record, you have a misplaced confidence that you will be able to recreate the original at any future date. Alas! this seldom turns out to be true. As the time of examination draws near only too often you will not be able to make head or tail of those lecture notes which you took down six months ago and have not looked at since—nor remember some crucial detail of that experiment which you omitted to write up on the day.

If you feel that merely going over the work again is too tedious an exercise, read another account of the same subject in a textbook, expanding your notes by additions and comments; for this purpose write your notes on one side of the paper only, to leave room for these additions.

The first revision, then, should take place as soon as possible after the original learning. Further revisions are often necessary before the final revision which precedes examinations. Consider those courses, like medicine and surgery, where mastery of the subject matter is literally a matter of life and death, and the pass mark may have to be set at 100 per cent. Nearly all medical schools give tests and examinations every few weeks, so that the students are continually revising their knowledge. In this way recall becomes mechanical and automatic. Such automation may be unnecessary or even undesirable in arts subjects, but there are probably aspects of most subjects, such as the grammar of foreign languages, or statistical formulae, which can well be so practised that their use becomes second nature to the subject. This is even more markedly true of physical skills such as typewriting or driving a car or swimming or hitting a golf ball, where the essence of skilled performance consists of reducing the skill to an automatic level. We take it for granted that physical skills develop gradually and demand repeated practice for their perfection. The same is true of some aspects of study.

In revision before examinations you should pay particular attention to the earlier material you have learnt, as more of it will have been forgotten. You should leave yourself time to go over all the material you have covered. Studies have shown that subjective estimates of strengths and weaknesses are often at fault. You are often weak on material which you are confident you know well.

Active revision, and a few attempts at answering old examination questions should give you a better idea of where your true strengths and weaknesses lie.

You will realize that the amount of time that you give to each of the steps of the SQ3R study technique will depend on the subjects you are studying. The natural sciences, the social sciences, the arts, and practical and vocational subjects differ in their aims and methods. The wide and discursive reading which is expected of students of English literature, for example, is not required in an applied science, where there is a basic core of facts and techniques which must be mastered before elementary competence can be reached. The SQ3R method can, however, be applied in principle to all fields of study. It is very like the famous steps of instruction of the nineteenth century German educationist, Herbart: preparation, presentation, association, generalization and application. Preparation includes our first two steps of survey and question, in which the aims of study are set out, and the learner is encouraged to marshal his present stock of knowledge. Presentation and association include the reading and recitation stages, rather more stress being put by Herbart on thinking and reflection than on sheer recitation as a means of uniting the new knowledge with the old. Herbart's final steps of generalization, that is the drawing of general truths and principles, and the application of knowledge to practice, need to be added to the SQ3R formula. If you are concerned, as you should be, not only to pass examinations, but to retain your knowledge for a working lifetime, and to put it to good use, you must attempt to reduce it to general principles, and to apply it in practice.

1770 words

Write down the time taken to read this passage and then turn over and answer the Tests.

COMPREHENSION TESTS

A. Retention

Do not refer back to the passage

1 List the five steps in the SQ3R study system.
2 What kind of reading is usually required on the first reading of a textbook chapter?
3 What might happen if you skip over graphs or tables when reading a textbook?
4 Who said, 'If you read anything over twenty times you will not learn it by heart so easily as if your were to read it only ten, trying to repeat it between whiles, and when memory failed looking at the book'?
5 What is meant by Recitation in the SQ3R study system?
6 Give two examples of learning mentioned by the writer when literal word-for-word recitation is applicable?
7 Which stage of the SQ3R study system could be described as 'making a reconnaissance before you start your main work and getting an over-all perspective of what lies before you'?
8 At which points in the reading of a textbook does the writer say you should 'lay the book on one side and try and recall what you have been reading'?
9 After how long do 'American studies suggest that typically the average student scores only about 30 per cent of the perfect score on a test of factual knowledge'?
10 The SQ3R study system is very similar to the famous steps of instruction of which nineteenth-century German educationist?

B. Understanding and Interpretation

Do not refer back to the passage

1 What can be inferred from the passage about the nature of critical reading?
2 Does the writer imply that recitation, in the sense of learning by heart, is generally useful, or not?
3 What evidence is there in the passage to suggest that the human memory does not operate in the same way as a computer's 'memory' in which information can be stored permanently on magnetic tape?
4 From your reading of the passage, would you say continuous revision, as recommended by the writer, most benefits the science student or the arts student?

5 Is the writer more concerned with enabling students to be successful in examinations or with helping them to make their studies of lasting benefit to themselves?

C. Discussion and Evaluation

You may refer back to the passage

1 What are the main differences between study-reading and other kinds of reading?
2 Discuss the values of a systematic approach to study. How many of us ever receive any training in the techniques of studying?
3 In what ways does the present examination system cause teachers to concentrate less on *educating* their students and more on *training* them to pass examinations?
4 Compare in detail SQ3R and your own approach to study. Indicate any useful conclusions this comparison enables you to draw.
5 Discuss the importance of 'recall' to comprehension.

Practice Work

Continue the practice work recommended at the end of Passage Five.

Passage Seven

Following the usual procedure, and attempting to improve your performance, turn over and begin reading.

Begin timing.

PASSAGE SEVEN

from *Personal Values in the Modern World* by M. V. C. Jeffreys

The problem of unifying our culture brings with it another problem—that of communication. A society cannot have a coherent culture—it cannot even have a coherent existence—unless there is effective communication among its members.

There are two main reasons for the contemporary interest in communication. One is the enormous development of the technical means of communication. The other is the fact that our national and international problems increasingly depend for their solution on effective communication, and our failure to solve them is largely due to failure of communication.

In these days no important problem is a local, self-contained problem. Our problems cannot be insulated, but involve increasingly complex interrelations. Food, clothes, and fuel, which in the pre-industrial society could be purely local problems, are world problems. Social groups, industrial organizations, nations and groups of nations, cannot ignore one another, something is likely to go wrong on a large scale.

The outstanding example of failure of communication is the great international barrier of the Iron Curtain. The deep distrust between East and West is the result of two fundamentally irreconcilable views of life. It is not a mere matter of diagreement; for disagreement presupposes that the parties have something in common to disagree about. It is rather a matter of two sets of assumptions which are so alien to one another as to preclude discussion. You cannot argue with people who, starting from different assumptions, do not know what you mean.

If we look within our own national borders, we must recognize that communication is hindered not only by the fragmentation of thought and knowledge which was described earlier, but also by the breaking-up of society itself into homogeneous groups out of touch with one another. One of the most important results of the Industrial Revolution has been the virtual disappearance of the old mixed community of the village or market town, in which all ranks of society shared traditions and customs and, to a large extent, a common life. The industrial town is an unpleasant place to live in, and improved transport enables those who can afford to live elsewhere to do so. Our social distribution has thus developed away from the old mixed community towards the one-class communities of slum, suburb, and (more recently) housing estates. Town planners have tried to re-create the mixed community; but their efforts are perhaps rather artificial. Meanwhile the impersonal character of large organizations (large industries, large public services) does not help to establish understanding between people. There is nothing more frustrating than trying to deal with an organization (local education authority, hospital, or telephone service) where one cannot get hold of anyone who will talk to one on a man-to-man basis. It is small wonder that the general public tend to accept, with passive docility, the treatment they receive from the organized social services. Impersonal treatment is in the long run more undermining to morale than hostility.

The problem of communication can be seen from two standpoints—from the sending end and from the receiving end.

On the one hand are those who, by ability and training, should be equipped to lead thought and set standards. Professor C. Wright Mills of Columbia University, in *The Causes of World War Three*, says that the intellectuals are cut off from the control of communication, encapsuled in their specialisms, out of touch with the world at large, and at the mercy of power groups who can use them as instruments of policy which the intellectuals have not determined. He urges that the intellectuals should try to repossess themselves of the cultural apparatus, including the mass media. In effect he is asking for a revival, in a modern context, of Plato's idea of the philosopher-king. The *Universities Quarterly* for Autumn 1959 was given up to a symposium on the place of the creative writer in the university. No very startling conclusions were reached. There was in fact little more than what *The Times* described as a 'guarded admission that for those who like teaching a university job is not incompatible with creation'. *The Times* suggested that we ought to go much further in the direction already opened up by the American universities; that is to say, we should 'support creative writers without exacting from them too precisely measured a pound of flesh'. After referring to the fact that for the past thirteen years Mr E. M. Forster had been an honorary fellow of King's, Cambridge, and that Mr W. H. Auden's duties as Professor of Poetry at Oxford are not very arduous, *The Times* went on: 'May not the moral be that writers ought to be employed more extensively in universities for the sake of their indirect rather than their academic influence?' It might be added that the same principle could apply to people who work for the films and radio as well as to writers of books. The important thing is that artists in language and other media whose work reaches and influences the general public should be recognized by and associated with universities. In that way it might be possible to establish some connexion in the public mind between the world of entertainment and the world of scholarship. In 1962, in addition to the examples mentioned above, four universities in Great Britain have established fellowships in literature, music, and fine arts, the purpose of which is to encourage creative work that will reach the general public. In one of these universities, fourteen people have held such fellowships since 1950. At least one other university plans to establish fellowships of this kind. Two universities have departments of drama, and two plan to have them. A few universities are engaged in research into the techniques and effects of television.

On the face of it there is a good deal to be said for Professor Wright Mills's view about the role of the intellectual. The trouble about the intellectuals, however, is that too few of them have any message for the general public. With ever-increasing specialization, fewer highly educated people have a whole view of life, or observations on life as a whole, to communicate. Nor does the intellectual find it easy to communicate to the general public anything from his special field of study. The restricted range and esoteric idiom of modern scholarship are a barrier to communication which—as some laudable examples show—needs determined effort to break through. Moreover, the scholar who tries to 'popularize' his subject is unlikely to arouse the enthusiasm of his academic colleagues.

The modern intellectual, who might be expected to play the role of Plato's philosopher-king in modern dress, is thus doubly handicapped. On the one hand he seldom has a whole view of life to communicate to the general public. On the other hand, even if he has a message for the general public, he is unlikely to be able to utter it in a way that ordinary people can understand. Here is the other side of the problem of communication. The kind of education which qualifies a 'leader of thought' tends to make him unintelligible to the man in the street. 'He doesn't talk our language.' Worse still, he is liable to be distrusted, even if his social origin was among the very people with whom he wants to communicate. He has been separated from them by his education, by the manners he has acquired, by the company he keeps. 'He's no longer one of us.'

It is one of the hazards of educational opportunity that an intelligent working-class boy may be estranged from his original social background, and yet not fully assimilated into his new milieu. With the increase of educational opportunity there has been coming into existence a new intelligentsia, sprung from comparatively humble origins and without much background of social confidence and security. They are highly intelligent but for the most part do not earn very much money or gain very much power. They are a main source of teachers for schools and for the newer universities. Their quality is high, but their influence does not compare with that of organized labour or the 'establishment'. Indeed they may be made use of by power-groups.

Those whose education ought to equip them to be leaders of thought have a double obligation to fulfil if they are to exert effective influence. In the first place they must think out a coherent view of life which can give meaning and purpose to the various forms of work and leisure. Secondly, they must study ways of sharing their thoughts with the general public—an activity which involves a sensitive awareness of what is going on (confusedly no doubt) in the minds of people at large.

This double task is not easy. We shall not begin to cope with it unless we can move a long way beyond the assumption, common in academic circles, that communication consists primarily of exposition. As a means of communication exposition has a limited range and function. The existentialists know very well that drama, fiction, and other forms of art are not only more potent than exposition but have a much more general appeal. We are scarcely beginning to realize the possibilities of the mass media as means of serious communication. One of the difficulties of our age is that, being an age of doubt and not an age of faith, it produces fiction and drama which are analytic rather than constructive. Much contemporary drama, both high-brow and middle-brow, is negative rather than positive.

If communication is not primarily a matter of exposition, neither is it primarily a matter of words. Words can obstruct communication, as everyone knows who has argued for an hour and a half only to discover at the end of it that the two parties were meaning different things by the same terms. Communication, indeed, is not primarily an intellectual activity: though intellectual activity, properly conducted, can greatly aid communication.

The basis of communication is shared feeling. And failure of communication is ultimately due to there being no common feeling or experience to share. Language barriers can usually be overcome between people who have a strong interest in common, whether it be bargaining, escaping or making love. But where the lives of people or groups of people do not touch at any point, there can be no communication. In this connexion it may be worth while to recall what was said earlier about the virtual disappearance of the pre-industrial mixed community, and the appearance in its place of the various one-class, one-type communities.

If, however, a common interest—such as gardening—can be found among a miscellaneous group of people (say a factory worker, a business executive, a smallholder, and a professor) communication will begin. Not only that, but communication, once begun, will spread to other topics as mutual confidence is established. Once people begin to trust one another, they will want to explore each other's minds and share their experience. To this end there is great value in voluntary social activities, such as dramatic societies, rambling clubs, Women's Institutes, and the like, which bring a varied assortment of people together for a clear and limited purpose, in the pursuit of which they can lose their self-consciousness. As they get to know one another better, they will make friends, widen their general experience of life, and find more things in common than the original object of association.

Experience is wider and more common than language. A professor of philosophy and a factory bench-worker may be quite unable to discuss, say, the problems of moral behaviour. But, provided neither party has had the edge taken off his natural perceptions by the attrition of civilized life, both will know in terms of living experience what the problems of moral behaviour are, and both will be able to respond to situations where courage and compassion are matched against oppression and greed.

The parables of Jesus of Nazareth were understood equally by his humblest listeners and by the scribes. The understanding of goodness and beauty is not restricted to an intellectual elite, nor has it to be 'intellectualized'. Moral and aesthetic judgement springs out of experience approached sensitively and is essentially an active response to an actual situation. The formation of principles is not a precondition, but a convenient sequel, of moral and aesthetic experience. The best moral or aesthetic education is that which, through suitable experience, stimulates sensitiveness and sympathy with others.

Natural man, however naive and untaught, wants to ask the important questions about life—What are we for? What are the things that matter most? What is the highest good? Comfort without effort, achievement irrespective of comfort, getting as much as possible, giving as much as possible, looking after Number One, losing ourselves in something more than self? The real problem of education at all levels is not to provide answers to questions but to get people to ask the important questions, and especially to reawaken those who have become incapable of asking any questions at all. To stimulate honest and resolute inquiry, at whatever cost to comfort and convenience, has always been the aim of the greatest teachers, from Socrates onwards.

A further truth about communication is that true communication is personal—and in two senses. In the first place communication is between persons conscious of themselves and of one another as persons. There is a mutuality in true communication, with an active, questioning attitude on each side. The word itself has the implication of shared discourse. Mass communication, in which people are passively receptive to impressions, is an impersonal affair, sedative rather than stimulating, and tends to break down rather than build up the individuality of those who are habitually exposed to it. If we stop to think, that is not what we really mean by communication.

Secondly, communication is personal in the sense that the deepest truths are manifested in persons and not in propositions. As Lord Lindsay put it: 'The question as to the nature of justice was one which it was natural for Socrates to ask, and impossible for him to answer...And so Plato has given the Republic this curious form, because he believed that Socrates in his person and his life offered the real answer to the questions he propounded, and which his teaching never solved. A great teacher does not merely preach his gospel: he is his gospel.'

These reflections may remind us of the supreme importance of maintaining and promoting relations between people at a truly personal level. Whenever the person-to-person relation is lost within a community, that community loses value and significance as an electric battery runs down.

2210 words

Write down the time taken to read this passage and then turn over and answer the Tests.

COMPREHENSION TESTS

A. Retention

Do not refer back to the passage

1 What is necessary before a society can have a coherent culture?
2 Give one of the two reasons given by the writer for the contemporary interest in communication.
3 What is the outstanding example of the failure of communication referred to by the writer?
4 What does the writer say has been one of the most important results of the Industrial Revolution?
5 For what purpose did four British universities establish, in 1962, fellowships in literature, music and fine arts?
6 Who, in the writer's view, might be expected to play the role of Plato's philosopher-king in modern dress?
7 What kind of fiction and drama does the writer say our age, being an age of doubt and not an age of faith, produces?
8 What does the writer say is the basis of communication?
9 Out of what does moral and aesthetic judgement spring?
10 The writer states that true communication is personal. What happens whenever the person-to-person relationship is lost within a community?

B. Understanding and Interpretation

Do not refer back to the passage

1 List the main points made by the writer in this passage.
2 In your own words, explain the following: encapsuled in their specialisms; popularize; leader of thought; the establishment; the basis of communication is shared feeling.
3 What can be inferred from the passage about the writer's attitudes towards (*a*) the mass media, (*b*) intellectuals, (*c*) industrial society, (*d*) religion.
4 Why do you think the writer attaches great importance to voluntary social activities?
5 Why do you think the writer wishes to see better communication between people as individuals?

C. Discussion and Evaluation

You may refer back to the passage

1 How far is the existence of 'The Iron Curtain' the result of a fundamental failure in communication between East and West?
2 Why has the gathering together of people in large industrial

towns and cities and the enormous development of the technical means of communication resulted, paradoxically, in an increasing inability of individuals to communicate with each other?

3 What is your opinion of the role of the intellectual in society?

4 'It is one of the hazards of educational opportunity that an intelligent working-class boy may be estranged from his original social background, and yet not fully assimilated into his new milieu.' Do you agree? What are class barriers? Do they exist? How far do they result from the inability of people from different social and educational backgrounds to communicate with each other and how far from real differences in the social and economic aims of the various classes?

5 'True communication is personal.' Do you agree? How can personal relationships be improved in a complex industrial society?

Practice Work

Continue the practice work recommended at the end of Passage Five.

Passage Eight

Following the usual procedure, and attempting to improve your performance, turn over and begin reading.

Begin timing.

PASSAGE EIGHT

from *Discrimination and Popular Culture* edited by Denys Thompson

Applied science has enormously increased the world's population. The extra people live mainly in large units that tend more and more to resemble each other. They have to be reached by their governments and by all the agencies that wish to impart news, opinions, and announcements of goods and services for sale. The town crier, the notice in the church porch, and the back-street printer have been replaced by the means—radio, popular press, and advertising—that technology has made possible. The next gifts of applied science to very large numbers of people were more leisure, more energy to enjoy it, and a much greater spending power. And as a result home-made amusements, live performances, and inexpensive hobbies are supplanted by a large and well-organized entertainment industry that reaches deeply into our homes and pockets. Much that used to be supplied locally is now centrally provided by newspapers, publicity, radio, film, records, magazines, and the mass-production of things used and enjoyed in the home.

The reformers of the nineteenth century nobly hoped that the workers, once freed from the prison of illiteracy and long hours, would give themselves a liberal education and feed on the same intellectual delights as the reformers themselves. Their disappointed hopes may have been pitched too high: today our expectations of popular culture seem altogether too low. The hypothesis of this book is that the shortcomings of popular culture are with us because the mass media just listed have become the expression and the mouthpiece of a particular type of civilization. One, that is, in which our productive powers have acquired a life of their own and run away with us. The drift can certainly be checked and society acquire a sense of direction, but up to the present changes seem to have been too swift for us fully to control them or successfully adapt ourselves to them. The mass media affect our lives closely at many points, perhaps more intimately than we are aware of. This book is an attempt by its authors to throw light upon this influence.

The pervasiveness of the media is made possible by mass-production, which gives us cheap and efficient printed matter and receiving-sets. The implications of mass-production are worth considering. It needs a great deal of capital. In oil refining, for instance, the cost of the plant per person employed is about £12,500; in chemicals it may reach £30,000. Thus idle plant can be ruinous; as far as possible it must be worked all day and every day. The same applies to the means of reaching people. Newspapers must circulate, not only to gain advertising, but to ensure that the capital locked up in forests and pulp-making shows a return. A Sunday paper may be started, not to meet a demand, but because it will occupy presses that would otherwise be unprofitably still. Again, the specialized machinery for producing paper-backs is so costly that it must be kept moving; and new techniques for printing text-books in colour involve so expensive a setting-up that 'it is not worth printing fewer than 100,000 or even 250,000 copies'. If we turn to the film industry, we find that an average film costs £150,000 in the two months it takes to make, and an exceptional one may need £3,000,000.

Much of what applies to the mass-production of goods is true also of the mass media. The people who handle the large capital invested are under an obligation to see that it shows a profit, so the media, or the plant which produces them, must be employed for as many hours of the twenty-four as possible. We might be better off if newspapers were smaller, paper-backs fewer, and television much reduced in quantity. But even if the controllers agreed, they could not do much about it; they are there to keep the machinery going. Quantity becomes more important than quality, and poor quality is concealed by dazzlingly efficient presentation.

Other features of mass-production are also found in the mass media. What is presented must be 'safe', unprovocative and generally acceptable. Individual preferences are ignored, because mass-production pays best when millions of copies of a few designs are turned out, rather than fewer copies of more designs. Thus mass communications 'exercise a constant pressure upon their users to invoke similar responses from the largest numbers of people'. At present the 'similar responses' tend to be at a low level, for the controllers generally aim at the lowest common factors to be found in the audience. Again, the sub-division of work that characterizes mass-production is found in films, radio, and pop music. In the latter, for example, we are told that 'the sole contribution of the composer is his ability to whistle a little tune which he is incapable of writing on paper. Then the skilled services of the arranger come into play...' Responsibility is divided till it ceases to exist.

Though the controllers of the media claim 'freedom' for their activities, they seem very much to be prisoners of the conditions we have described. As long as they aim merely at big audiences, so long will their behaviour be predictable. While the market is the test of what shall be disseminated, the controllers appear to be the tools of impersonal forces, and in their subservience they are bound to provide us with worse fare than we deserve or the media are capable of. Their apology for their present practice is that they 'give the public what it wants', and they interpret the acquiescence of the public as positive approval. But without good reason. Very few indeed of the readers of popular newspapers, for example, would applaud the ruthless and inhuman methods of the reporters who intrude on grief, extract 'reactions' from distressed people, betray confidences. The things are done because the controllers think they ought to be done. Most of us again may have a streak of the ghoul within us, which we usually subordinate to better impulses. But in the conditions imposed on them editors and reporters see all their readers as ghouls if there are corpses available. The controllers in sum have no vital contact with their audience; they are ignorant of its composition and history; they cannot see people for TAM ratings and ABC figures.

According to the controllers, the masses do not want to learn; they want only to be entertained. But (as the late J. Trenaman commented after some years' work on television) there is no research or evidence to support such a view, whereas there is evidence to the contrary. If the controllers are right, then people like being sold rubbish and enjoy being deceived by advertising. Both selling rubbish and deception are widespread, according to the 'Molony' Report, but they continue because the consumer accepts his disappointment philosophically or puts it down to his own misjudgement. Something of the kind happens with the mass media; 'giving the public what it wants' turns out to mean disposing of goods or entertainment that will vaguely satisfy a large number of people, without prompting active interest or approval. As Lord Hailsham said of television:

> 'The TAM rating can be, I think sometimes is, a melancholy record of third and fourth preferences—the maximum number of viewers who can be induced not to turn off, the highest common factor of endurance without enthusiasm.'

Even if the controllers were able to establish in a particular case that there was a genuine preference for what they supply, they would almost certainly be found to have created the taste for it. For what sells most is not necessarily the best product or the best value for money; it is more likely to be the most efficiently publicized and pushed. As Mr Farr so convincingly shows, the sales of a product are by no means an indication of what the consumer wants. The overriding concern of the controllers is profit, and they naturally manipulate the public taste if they can. The extent of their power can be over-estimated—there is not enough evidence, for one rarely comes across so revealing a statement as that made by H. Ratcliffe, of the Musicians' Union. Discussing popular music and records, he said:

'Any music publisher can tell you six months ahead which tune is going to be popular. The public does not make a tune popular. Subject to certain exceptions, some flukes here and there, we know in advance what is going to be popular six months ahead, and the publishing business makes sure a tune it wants to be popular is popular, by spending enough money to make it popular.'

Characteristically the controllers, wielding power without true responsibility over audiences they never meet, despise them. Only contempt can account for the quality of some of the offerings. One can sense it in many an advertisement and commercial, and perhaps in this reported quotation from Cecil King, Chairman of Daily Mirror Newspapers, Ltd: 'In point of fact it is only the people who conduct newspapers and similar organizations who have any idea quite how indifferent, quite how stupid, quite how uninterested in education of any kind the great bulk of the British public are.' A different point of view is put by Arnold Wesker:

'It is the age of the big insult—trivia pays larger dividends, therefore trivia must be what is wanted. Is this a deliberate policy to keep the nation cretinized by trivialities or does it stem from a profound belief that the people of this country are cretins from the start?'

Owing to their cynicism and ignorance of the variety and resources of their audiences, the controllers are sometimes astoundingly inept in deciding and arranging what shall be consumed— despite all the slickness of presentation. And the freedom they talk about is one-sided. There can be no freedom for viewer or reader without choice; and people can make a real choice only if they have a more than superficial acquaintance with the possibilities. This knowledge of the range of things to choose from is just what the controllers in general do not find it possible to supply. The hunt for mass audiences, needed to attract advertising or pay for it, causes the controllers to narrow the field of taste in which people can discriminate; 'they will be kept unaware of what lies beyond the average of experience'.

We exist as a nation to produce more goods. That is the answer one would get from a spokesman for any political party. Increased production is the common cry, with small mention of the nature and quality and destination of what is to be produced. It seems odd to anyone who thinks back a generation, or so. The need then was to produce more so that no one should go without; easier times were just round the corner. We have rounded the corner and—with some exceptions—no one need go without in a welfare state. But we are still incited to produce more, to keep up with neighbours at home or abroad. Not yet is the worker allowed to enjoy the fruits of his labour in leisure. Most workers now have more than their grandfathers would have thought enough. The basic needs are fulfilled, but fresh ones are constantly being created by advertising; and leisure is now to be regarded, under the same pressure, as an opportunity to spend on advertised goods and services. One example of the fresh needs is the extension of one sex's habits to the other. The effort has been made to make drinking in pubs respectable for girls and women, while for men it is no longer effeminate to use scent, provided it is sold as after-shave lotion.

Some of the best comments on the process are made by Professor J. K. Galbraith. Observing that 'one cannot defend production as satisfying wants if that production creates the wants', he continues:

'Were it so that a man on arising each morning was assailed by demons which instilled in him a passion sometimes for silk shirts, sometimes for kitchenware, sometimes for chamber-pots, and sometimes for orange squash, there would be every reason to applaud the effort to find the goods, however odd, that quenched this flame. But should it be that his passion was the result of his first having cultivated the demons, and should it be also that his effort to allay it stirred the demons to even greater and greater effort, there would be question as to how rational was his solution...He might wonder if the solution lay with more goods or fewer demons...Production only fills a void that it has itself created.'

The charge against advertising that it distorts a nation's economy was first made a good many years ago, and Professor Galbraith enlarges it with a wealth of example, stressing especially private affluence with public poverty. Such opinions may be very important, but they do not get much of a hearing in press and radio for:

'With the exception of the BBC the mass media are part of this process—production for its own sake. Advertising, broadcasting, and the Press make the consumer goods seem indispensable for happiness. Films and magazines work closely with them to glorify the consuming life. Records tax the leisure that might otherwise pay too small a tribute, and a host of goods of indifferent design and quality multiply the occasions for spending and display.'

It may be said that there is nothing very dreadful in all this, though the creation of artificial wants to be satisfied by consumer goods is hardly a satisfactory aim for society. The controllers supply entertainment which more or less contents a good many people, and why should anyone worry? But of course there is very little 'pure' entertainment. The individual's capacity for thought and feeling is being strengthened or weakened all the time by what he sees and hears, and his views (about the social order, for instance) may derive entirely from entertainment. 'Entertainment' is much of it a form of propaganda for things as they are, relentlessly pressing us to be good conformers and avid consumers. Again, however good entertainment may be, it must at present be an occasion for spending and a means of profit to somebody. This condition excludes all sorts of civilized diversions.

Members of the 1960 Conference felt there was more to it than entertainment. The most noticeable thread running through the proceedings was the express hostility of teachers towards the way in which the mass media are used at present. For example: 'There is bound to be a very sharp conflict between the task of education and the role of the media, which are still closely linked to securing profit and to the advertising industry' (Stuart Hall). The feeling was so strong that the word 'media' was evidently felt to be a misnomer; they were not just vehicles for transmitting views and entertainment—they provided the views, filtered the news, and devised a special kind of entertainment. As Abrams demonstrates so clearly, those who operate the channels decide what shall flow through them. They have created the taste, often entirely new in scale and often in kind, for what they supply to their public. All the same, it is pointless to isolate the mass media in the dock; rather should we look critically at the civilization in which the offerings of the entertainment industry are necessary and acceptable.

'The selves we are are to a great extent the product of our social contacts.' It may be that these social contacts are being replaced by the mass media; what they supply for us to read and hear and see may influence us decisively. Our national culture is being replaced by a synthetic substance that exists only in the media. For instance, no one outside an agency ever talks like an advertisement; and the attitudes of the popular press are rarely a crystallization of what any of their readers feel, just as the language in which the news is conveyed is a special one never spoken in real life. The 'midatlantic' speech of entertainers and others exists at present only on radio and television, though doubtless it will soon spread thence. Television in particular is seen by some observers to be the agent of moral and aesthetic education, supplying a continuous stream of attitude-forming information under the label of entertainment, replacing the teaching of church and family and school. So that:

'Faced with this kind of pressure the responsibility of the teacher becomes very great. Matched against the glib facility of a radio commentator supported by all the gimmicks and aids to presentation, the classroom teacher is gravely hampered in an age in which the titillation of public fancy has become a matter of professional expertise. His influence on adolescent minds has to be weighed against that of ephemeral stars of film or T.V. screen. The easy success of popular entertainers is in great contrast to the sustained effort needed to achieve anything worth while in other spheres—and especially in the school.'

Year Book of Education, 1960

If the criticisms, on educational grounds, of the industry are valid, teachers are wasting their time. Children are taught to read —up to a point; they leave school with the ability to skim the surface of advertisements and newspapers and magazines. Nowadays this is not enough: children need not only to be given a tool, but taught how to use it. Teachers are not to blame if their pupils are less than half-educated, for schools are still organized to prepare entrants to industry instead of providing education for life.

2750 words

Write down the time taken to read this passage and then turn over and answer the Tests.

COMPREHENSION TESTS

A. Retention

Do not refer back to the passage

1 Name two means of communication that radio, newspapers and advertising have replaced.
2 What was the noble hope of the reformers of the nineteenth century?
3 What makes the pervasiveness of the mass media possible?
4 What does the average film cost to make?
5 What is the result of mass-production as far as the mass media are concerned?
6 What was Cecil King's view of the bulk of the British public?
7 What was the charge against advertising referred to by the writer?
8 How does the writer describe much of 'entertainment'?
9 How does the writer describe the attitude of teachers at the 1960 conference towards the way in which the mass media are used at present?
10 Why, in the writer's opinion, are teachers not to blame if their pupils are less than half-educated?

B. Understanding and Interpretation

Do not refer back to the passage

1 What, do you infer, is the writer's attitude towards the mass media?
2 Why do you think 'we might be better off if newspapers were smaller, paper-backs fewer, and television much reduced in quantity'?
3 Why must what is presented by the mass media be 'safe, unprovocative and generally acceptable'?
4 What inferences can be made about the way in which the writer thinks reading skills should be taught in schools?
5 *In your own words,* explain the following: liberal education; Responsibility is divided till it ceases to exist; trivia; 'pure' entertainment; 'The selves we are are to a great extent the product of our social contacts'.

C. Discussion and Evaluation

You may refer back to the passage

1 How far do you agree or disagree with the writer's central thesis that the mass media of communication have a harmful influence on our society?

64

2 What is 'popular culture' (*a*) as you think the writer understands it and (*b*) as you understand it?

3 How far do you agree or disagree with Cecil King? Did your agreement or disagreement affect in any way your acceptance or rejection of the points the writer makes in this passage?

4 Are schools 'still organized to prepare entrants to industry instead of providing education for life'? Discuss the implication of the word 'still' in this context.

5 What do you consider *should be* the purposes and functions of the mass media in contemporary society?

Practice Work

Continue the practice recommended at the end of Passage Five.

Passage Nine

Following the usual procedure, and attempting to improve your performance, turn over and begin reading.

Begin timing.

PASSAGE NINE

The BBC's Duty to Society by Sir Hugh Greene

The main purpose of broadcasting is to make the microphone and the television screen available to the widest possible range of subjects and to the best exponents available of the differing views on any given subject: to let the debate decide—or not decide as the case may be—and, in Cardinal Heenan's words, 'to emerge with a deeper knowledge'.

An atmosphere of healthy scepticism

The presentation of varying views does not mean that the BBC merely seeks to foster an equivocal attitude towards all that it broadcasts; to attach a ubiquitous, unanswered question-mark to everything it touches, in religion, culture, politics or education. But it does mean, in my opinion, that the BBC should encourage the examination of views and opinions in an atmosphere of healthy scepticism. I say 'healthy scepticism' because I have a very strong personal conviction that scepticism is a most healthy frame of mind in which to examine accepted attitudes and test views which, in many cases, have hitherto been accepted too easily—or too long. Perhaps what is needed, ideally (though we cannot all—I certainly cannot—achieve the ideal) is what T. S. Eliot described as 'an ability to combine the deepest scepticism with the profoundest faith'.

It follows that in its search for truth—indeed, in whatever it undertakes—a broadcasting organization must recognize an obligation towards tolerance and towards the maximum liberty of expression. As John Milton put it 300 years ago, in one of the most famous essays in the English language against censorship and in favour of freedom of expression:

'Where there is much desire to learn, there of necessity will be much arguing, many opinions; for opinion in good men is but knowledge in the making.'

The BBC operates under one of the least restricting legal instruments known in Britain, namely a Royal Charter, supported by a licence to operate from the Postmaster-General. These two instruments lay down a relatively small number of things which the BBC must *not* do. It must not carry advertisements or sponsored programmes. It must not express its own opinions about current affairs or matters of public policy. Almost the only positive thing which the Corporation is required to do is to broadcast daily an impartial account of the proceedings of Parliament—and even that the BBC started to do on its own initiative, before it was made an obligation. For the rest, the BBC is left to conduct its affairs to the broad satisfaction of the British people (and in the last analysis, of Parliament) under the guidance and legal responsibility of its Governors.

Freedom and responsibility

Of course, again like Britain itself, over the years a number of conventions have grown up which—almost with the force of law but not quite—govern the BBC's conduct in practice. Unlike, for example, theatres in Britain (which are subject to the censorship of a high official of the royal court), and unlike the cinema (which is subject to censorship by a self-established cinema industry board of censors and also to the rulings of local magistrates), the BBC is subject only to its own self-control and, naturally, to the laws of the country. These laws are especially severe in a field which is of especial concern to all broadcasters and newspapermen—the law of defamation. But subject to these few restrictions the BBC, its Governors, and Director-General are left alone to keep for themselves the delicate balance between freedom and responsibility.

How do we in the BBC interpret and use this freedom? Straight away I should say we do not see this freedom as total licence. We have (and believe strongly in) editorial control. Producers of individual programmes are not simply allowed to do whatever they like. Lines must be drawn somewhere. But, in an operation as diverse in its output as broadcasting, the only sure way of exercising control—here we come to one of my personal beliefs—is to proceed by persuasion and not by written directives; by encouraging the programme staff immediately responsible to apply their judgment to particular problems, within a framework of general guidance arising from the continuing discussion of individual programmes by their seniors—by, that is, the BBC's senior executives and, when necessary, by the Board of Governors. In my view there is nothing to be achieved by coercion or censorship, whether from inside the Corporation or from outside—nothing, that is, except the frustration of creative people who can achieve far more by positive stimulation of their ideas in an atmosphere of freedom.

67

The new attempts at censorship

In stimulating these ideas we have to take account of several important factors, some of which are new to this age of broadcasting, some of which are as old as articulate man himself. We have to resist attempts at censorship. As Professor Richard Hoggart has noted recently, these attempts at censorship come not merely from what he describes as the old 'guardians' (senior clergy, writers of leading articles in newspapers, presidents of national voluntary organizations) who like to think of themselves as upholders of cultural standards although, in many cases, they lack the qualities of intellect and imagination to justify that claim. The attempts at censorship come nowadays also from groups—Hoggart calls them the 'new populists'—which do not claim to be 'guardians' but claim to speak for 'ordinary decent people' and claim to be 'forced to take a stand against' *unnecessary* dirt, *gratuitous* sex, *excessive* violence—and so on. These 'new populists' will attack whatever does not underwrite a set of prior assumptions, assumptions which are anti-intellectual and unimaginative. Superficially this seems like a 'grass-roots' movement. In practice it can threaten a dangerous form of censorship—censorship which works by causing artists and writers not to take risks, not to undertake those adventures of the spirit which must be at the heart of every truly new creative work.

Such a censorship is the more to be condemned when we remember, that, historically, the greatest risks have attached to the maintenance of what is right and honourable and true. Honourable men who venture to be different, to move ahead of—or even against—the general trend of public feeling, with sincere conviction and with the intention of enlarging the understanding of our society and its problems, may well feel the scourge of public hostility many times over before their worth is recognized. It is the clear duty of a public-service broadcasting organization to stand firm against attempts to decry sincerity and vision, whether in the field of public affairs or in the less easily judged world of the arts including the dramatic art.

I believe that broadcasters have a duty not to be diverted by arguments in favour of what is, in fact, disguised censorship. I believe we have a duty to take account of the changes in society, to be ahead of public opinion rather than always to wait upon it. I believe that great broadcasting organizations, with their immense powers of patronage for writers and artists, should not neglect to cultivate young writers who may, by many, be considered 'too advanced', even 'shocking'. Such allegations have been made throughout the ages. Many writers have been condemned as sub- versive when first published. Henrik Ibsen, for example, was at one time regarded as too shocking for his plays to be staged in Britain. At least in the secular and scientific fields, today's heresies often prove to be tomorrow's dogmas. And, in the case of the potential Ibsens of today, we must not, by covert censorship, run the risk of stifling talents which may prove great before they are grown.

Programme plans

I do not need to be reminded that broadcasting has access to every home, and to an audience of all ages and varying degrees of sophis- tication. We must rely, therefore, not only on our own disciplines but on those which have to be exercised by, among others, parents. Programme plans must, to my mind, be made on the assumption that the audience is capable of reasonable behaviour, and of the exercise of intelligence—and of choice. No other basis will meet the needs of the situation. How *can* one consciously plan for the unreasonable or the unintelligent? It is impossible, or if not strictly speaking impossible, utterly disastrous.

Editorial discretion must concern itself with two aspects of the content of broadcasting—subjects and treatments. If the audience is to be considered as it really is—as a series of individual minds (each with its own claim to enlightenment, each of different capacity and interests) and not as that statistical abstraction the 'mass' audience—then it would seem to me that no subject can be ex- cluded from the range of broadcasting simply for being what it is. The questions which we must face are those of identifying the times and the circumstances in which we may expect to find the intended audience for a given programme.

Relevance is the key—relevance to the audience, and to the tide of opinion in society. Outrage is wrong. Shock may not be good. Provocation can be healthy and indeed socially imperative. These are the issues to which the broadcaster must apply his conscience. But treatment of the subject, once chosen, demands the most care- ful assessment of the reasonable limits of tolerance in the audience, if there is any likelihood of these limits being tested by the manner of presentation of the material. As I have said, however, no subject is (for me) excluded simply for what it is.

The Pilkington Committee

The Pilkington Committee described the responsibilities of broadcasting in these matters, like this. Broadcasting, it said,

> 'must pay particular attention to those parts of the range of worthwhile experience which lie beyond the most common: to those parts which some have explored here and there, but few everywhere. Finally, and of special importance: because the growing points are usually most significant, it is on these that broadcasting must focus a spotlight.'

Does all this, I wonder, sound arrogant? What right have I and my colleagues in the BBC—even with the guidance of our Board of Governors—to decide where lines should be drawn? Why should we be more wise than outside censors? I don't suppose we always are more wise. But—here we come to another of my personal convictions and one which I think one can support from the experience of history—it is better to err on the side of freedom than of restriction.

Attempts at both open and disguised forms of censorship are only one of the forms of pressure to which the BBC, like all other independent broadcasting organizations, is subject. In the case of the BBC, however, we are especially fortunate in our power to resist. Some governments, of course, can and do exercise pressure. What may happen in various parts of the world where programmes are broadcast under the commercial (sponsorship) system is perhaps somewhat less familiar. A former Chairman of the American Federal Communications Commission, Mr Newton Minow, has described a classic example of such pressures. The gas industry (he recalled) sponsored the presentation in a drama series of a play about the Nuremberg war trials, under the title 'Judgment at Nuremberg'. Viewers noticed that a speech by actor Claude Rains about the killing through cyanide gas of thousands of concentration camp prisoners was abruptly interrupted by a deletion of words. The editing was done by a television network engineer while the video-tape recording of the drama was actually on the air. The words eliminated were 'gas chamber'. The editing was done to accommodate the gas industry sponsor; and a broadcasting company executive later gave this explanation: '...We felt that a lot of people could not differentiate between the kind of gas you put in the death chambers and the kind you cook with...'

One of American television's finest writers, Rod Serling, has also recounted the changes in a script that an advertising agency can force. Mr Serling based a one-hour drama on the lynching of a Negro boy in the deep South. By the time the agency had finished with the story, the chief character was a former convict, and living not even in the South but in New England!

Nor can we on this side of the Atlantic afford to be smug about the dangers. Our own post-bag of correspondence at the BBC is full of examples of attempts to exercise pressure in favour of this interest or against that—usually by complaints or by thinly disguised threats to cause trouble by approaches to Members of Parliament.

Truth, accuracy, and impartiality

Without true independence, therefore, it is difficult for any broadcaster to maintain the highest standards of truth, accuracy, and impartiality. Conversely, without a reputation for these things— truth, accuracy, and impartiality—it is difficult for any broadcasting organization to be recognized as truly independent and to be generally trusted. Truth and accuracy are concepts which are not susceptible of legal definition. The Government is content to recognize that the BBC tries to honour these concepts, and to treat 'with due impartiality' all controversial subjects. But although, in the day-to-day issues of public life, the BBC tries to attain the highest standards of impartiality, there are some respects in which it is not neutral, unbiased, or impartial. That is, where there are clashes for and against the basic moral values—truthfulness, justice, freedom, compassion, tolerance, for example.

Nor do I believe that we should be impartial about certain things, like racialism or extreme forms of political belief. Being too good 'democrats' in these matters could open the way to the destruction of our democracy itself. I believe a healthy democracy does not evade decisions about what it can never allow if it is to survive. The actions and aspirations of those who proclaim some political and social ideas are so clearly damaging to society, to peace and good order, even in their immediate effects, that to put at their disposal the enormous power of broadcasting would be to conspire with them against society.

2180 words

Write down the time taken to tead this passage and then turn over and answer the Tests.

COMPREHENSION TESTS

A. Retention

Do not refer back to the passage

1 What, in the writer's opinion, is the main purpose of broadcasting?
2 In what kind of atmosphere should the BBC encourage the examination of views and opinions?
3 Name the two 'instruments' under which the BBC operates.
4 What is almost the only positive thing which the BBC is required to do?
5 To what form of censorship is the BBC subjected?
6 Name two kinds of people whom Richard Hoggart has described as the old 'guardians'?
7 For whom do the 'new populists' claim to speak?
8 Which great dramatist does the writer state was at one time regarded as too shocking for his plays to be staged in Britain?
9 What example does the writer quote of the kind of censorship to which commercial (sponsorship) broadcasting systems may be subject?
10 On what kind of controversial issue does the writer think the BBC should *not* be impartial?

B. Understanding and Interpretation

Do not refer back to the passage

1 What is the writer's attitude towards the 'new populists'?
2 Explain the following *in your own words*: healthy scepticism; to proceed by persuasion and not by written directives; 'ordinary decent people'; a 'grass-roots' movement; 'with due impartiality'.
3 What is the writer's attitude towards the censorship of broadcasting?
4 In what way are the assumptions of the 'new populists' 'anti-intellectual and unimaginative'?
5 At whom do you infer the last sentence in the passage is directed?

C. Discussion and Evaluation

You may refer back to the passage

1 How far should broadcasting be censored? (What is censorship? disguised censorship?)
2 What, in your opinion, is the purpose of broadcasting?

3 How far do you agree or disagree with the opinions Sir Hugh Greene expresses? How far do you feel you have been influenced by any preconceived ideas you may have had on this subject?

4 Watch a television play and then attempt a critical evaluation of it, bearing in mind the passage you have just read.

5 Plan what you consider to be an ideal evening's television. How far has the passage influenced you in preparing your plans? What other considerations did you bear in mind?

Practice Work

Continue the practice work recommended at the end of Passage Five.

Passage Ten

Following the usual procedure, and reading this passage *at what you now regard as a normal, comfortable speed*, turn over and begin reading.

So that you can compare your performance on this passage with your performance on Passage One, *do not skim or pre-read this passage*.

Begin timing.

PASSAGE TEN

from *Communications* by Raymond Williams

Because of the importance the institutions of communication now have in our society, we should include the teaching of certain basic facts about them in all our education. This should include something of their history and current social organization. It should include also some introduction to the ways in which they actually work.

The large impersonal media, such as the Press, the cinema, radio and television, come through to most people almost as acts of God. It is very difficult, without direct experience of their actual working, to see them as the products of men like ourselves. I know that since I have seen something of television and radio production, and of publishing, I have quite different attitudes to their finished work. It is a loss of naivety but also in many ways a gain in respect: more critical, in every good sense, because more informed. If we are to feel that our communication system belongs to the society, instead of feeling that it is what 'they' have set up for us, this kind of understanding of method must grow.

To follow through the real process in producing a newspaper, a magazine, a book, a radio discussion programme, a television play, a film, a hit-tune, an opera, is usually exciting and invariably educative. Much more of this could be done by an intelligent use of modern resources. The only danger to avoid is the quite common substitute for this work, in the glamorized 'public relations' version of all these activities which is now so often put out. If it is to be valuable, this kind of teaching must base itself on the methods of education and not of publicity especially since all our cultural institutions now suffer from the effects of this glamorized version, not only on others but on the people working in the tension between the glamour and the reality.

Teaching criticism

That education should be critical of all cultural work is often the first point that springs to mind. Criticism is certainly essential, but for a number of reasons we have often done it so badly that there has been real damage. It is wholly wrong, for example, if education is associated with criticism while the non-educational world is associated with practice. Personal practice, direct experience of the arts, understanding of the institutions, should all come first. Or rather, criticism should develop as an aspect of each of these kinds of teaching, for it will always be bad if it is really separated from them. In teaching 'the classics' we are usually not critical enough. We often substitute a dull and inert 'appreciation' which nobody can go on believing in for long. But then in teaching or commenting on all other work, we are usually so confident and so fierce that it is difficult to believe we are the same people. 'All that muck in the cinemas and on television' too often follows the routine remarks on the charm of the *Essays of Elia*, and neither does anybody any good.

Our real purpose should be to bring all cultural work within the same world of discourse: to see the connexions between Elia and the manufactured television personality as well as the difference in value between *Lord Jim* and *Captain Condor*. We have to learn confidence in our own real opinions, and this depends on a kind of openness and flexibility, from the beginning, which much academic criticism does nothing to help. It will only ever be real criticism if the process by which judgements are arrived at is shared by all those who are expected to underwrite the judgements or take them over. We can be certain that some of the judgements will not be agreed. But that is all right, for as the argument continues we learn what real criticism is.

Nearly all of us need help in seeing and judging the vast amount of work which comes our way. In education, we must be prepared to look at the bad work as well as the good. The principle in the past has been that once you know the good you can distinguish the bad. In fact this depends on how well you know the good, how well and personally you know why it is good, and how close the bad work is, in form, to anything you have learned to discuss.

I am sure that we are neglecting the world of ordinary communication to which all of us, after education, go home or go on. Yet this has crucial bearings on the whole social process which education is supposed to prepare us for. There are many ways of including this ordinary world. For example:

(i) Regular comparative reading of the range of national newspapers, with a look at headlines and with some detailed comparison of particular stories.

(ii) Discussion of the range of comics, with a detailed look at some kinds of story and drawing, and comparison with relevant stories in books and with stories and essays on similar topics written by pupils. For example, stories about schools in comics could be compared with one or two of the traditional school stories, with contemporary stories such as Jim Starling, and with 'before and after' school stories by pupils. As a guide to this, Orwell's essay on 'Boys' Weeklies' might be read and discussed. Or the fairly common 'rebel' stories in comics might be discussed in relation to Huckleberry Finn.

(iii) Discussion of advertisements of a particular commodity, alongside one of the *Which?* reports on the same commodity. The commodity could then be used and pupils could write their own reports on it.

(iv) Discussion of selected stories in women's and teenagers' magazines. At a later stage these could be compared, in terms of their implicit values, with the replies to those seeking advice in the same magazines.

(v) A comparative study of 'social images' of particular kinds of profession. For example, compare the version of 'the scientist' or 'the professor' in comics, in science-fiction stories, and in television programmes in which actual scientists appear. Other professions offering relevant material are policemen and detectives (over the whole range from comics and magazines to crime films and plays and documentaries), doctors and nurses, teachers, artists. Varying images of the criminal could also be compared, from a wide range of communications material. The social image of trade unionists could also be looked at, with material from films, television plays, television and radio interviews, and comparative newspaper reports on a particular dispute or strike.

(vi) Comparative visual studies of kinds of modern architecture and design, of the results of town planning and unplanned development, of 'before and after' appearance where an area has been redeveloped.

(vii) Regular discussion of two or three comparable television programmes, of a popular kind, e.g., Westerns or panel games.

(viii) Repeat sessions of such programmes as 'Juke Box Jury' with the inclusion of some different but still comparable music.

(ix) Writing reviews of current films, and then comparing them with published reviews, with publicity material, and with recordings of broadcast reviews.

I have done some work along these lines with adult and young-workers groups. I have been very much struck by the way in which, particularly with young workers, ideas for new kinds of study have come from the groups, once the work has been started. Any educational programme of this kind should be sufficiently flexible to allow these new issues to be followed up.

Two general points need emphasis. First, it is unreasonable to ask teachers to do this often difficult work without offering them training in it. The teaching of communications is now sufficiently important to become a regular part of training college work. A good deal of scattered material and experiment is ready to draw on, but needs co-ordination in relation to training. Two kinds of body are urgently required: a Communications Centre with a staff able to supply catalogues of existing material and to collect and prepare new material, particularly in the expensive visual fields; and an Institute of Communications Research, at university level, undertaking long-range research and analysis. If these bodies existed, links with teachers and with training colleges could easily be arranged. Meanwhile, the supply of facilities to teachers willing to undertake this work, and the support necessary in its early stages, are the responsibility of local education authorities who are already very willing to assume it.

Second, it is clear that the addition of this work to existing curricula raises many problems of time. But we have to ask ourselves, in view of the importance of modern communications in society, and of their sometimes oblique relation to education itself, not whether we can afford to give the time but whether we can afford not to give it. The work can be done at all stages of education, but it is perhaps particularly important in adolescence: in the leaving years especially, for it is then that the conflict between the values of school and the values of the adult world is most obvious. There is no need, however, for the work to be confined to schools. It should be a central part of the new liberal studies courses in technical colleges, and of apprentice courses. It should form a main part of informal work in the youth service, and it should be a normal subject—it is already increasing—in adult education. We should also remember that a lot of this work can be done through the large communications services themselves: both in general programmes and as part of the now expanding educational programmes. This is particularly important, not only because it can often be done so well in such services as television and radio (though parts of the work will always require the small class), but also because we misconceive the problem if we set education against the major communications systems. There is much in them to criticize, but there is also much to praise. There are many producers already anxious to do this kind of work, both as a part of direct education and because they know how much their own opportunities for doing valuable work depend on the development of an informed, unprejudiced, critical public. In the present very important stage of expansion, it is vital that the many responsible people in communications should work as closely as possible with the educational services, and that teachers and educational administrators (who have often been prejudiced about the newer communication forms, frequently with good if partial reasons) should make a real effort to reciprocate.

1700 words

Write down the time taken to read this passage and then turn over and answer the Tests.

COMPREHENSION TESTS

A. Retention

Do not refer back to the passage

1 What kind of basic facts should we teach about the institutions of communication?
2 What caused the writer to change his attitudes to the finished work of the large impersonal media?
3 What do we often substitute for a critical approach in teaching 'the classics'?
4 What has been the principle in the past in teaching criticism?
5 Name two of the ways suggested by the author of including the world of ordinary communication in teaching criticism.
6 With which kinds of students has the author 'done some work along these lines'?
7 What would be the work of the Communications Centre proposed by the writer?
8 What would be the work of the writer's proposed Institute of Communications Research?
9 The teaching of understanding of modern communications can be done at all stages of education, but at which stage is it particularly important?
10 Who does the writer allege have often been prejudiced about the newer communication forms?

B. Interpretation

Do not refer back to the passage

1 List the main points made by the writer in the passage.
2 How would you describe the writer's attitude to teachers and educational administrators, 'who have often been prejudiced about the newer communication forms'?
3 What are the implications of what the writer says in this passage?
4 What is the writer's opinion of the way in which we teach 'the classics'?
5 Explain in your own words what you understand by the following as they are used in the passage: 'public relations'; the world of ordinary communication; 'social images'; the conflict between the values of school and the values of the adult world; an informed, unprejudiced, critical public?

C. Discussion and Evaluation

You may refer back to the passage

1 Why are the institutions of communication so important in our society now?

2 Assess the extent to which you, personally, have been taught to approach all cultural work critically.

3 Take *one* of the ways of 'including this ordinary world' of communication in assisting young people towards making sound judgements, and assess its effect on the improvement of critical skills.

4 Who is more to blame for the apparent conflict between the aims of education and the aims of the mass media? Teachers and educational administrators or those responsible for directing the mass media, or all of us?

5 How far do you agree or disagree with the points the writer makes? Did these agreements or disagreements influence you unduly in answering any of these questions?

CONCLUSION

Compare your performance on Passage Ten with your performance on Passage One. You should notice marked improvements. If you require a more precise calculation of the extent of the improvement in percentage terms use the following formula:

$$\text{percentage change} = \frac{(B-A)}{A} \times 100$$

(where A = Score on Passage One; B = Score on Passage Ten).

Your percentage improvement in reading speed should be between 80 and 120 per cent. If it is below this figure, you probably need further practice for a few more weeks. If it is above this, you have done very well but you should check to see that your comprehension has not suffered. If it has, you have probably tried to achieve too much too soon. Spend a few weeks on further practice work to consolidate your gains and to enable your comprehension to rise back to its previous level. It will.

You should not regard this point as the end of your training in reading. Whatever your achievements at this point you should continue, in your normal reading, trying to increase your reading speed gradually and should at the same time try to develop your ability to read critically and with understanding. It is certain that you will not have reached the peak of your personal efficiency in reading simply by working through the passages in this book. Considerable improvements, particularly in retention and understanding, lie ahead and only continued interest on your part and a continuing desire to improve will enable you to achieve them.

NOTES FOR TEACHERS USING THIS
BOOK WITH GROUPS

This section is particularly designed to help teachers, who have not previously given courses in the improvement of reading skills to their students, to avoid wasteful 'trial and error' methods in the construction and organization of courses.

A. Preparation

The essential instruction which the teacher needs to give his students can be found in any of the following books:

Teaching Faster Reading by Dr Edward Fry, Cambridge University Press, 1963.

Efficiency in Reading: a report on reading efficiency courses held at the Hull College of Technology by G. R. Wainwright, Dock Leaves Press, 1965.

Read Better, Read Faster by Manya and Eric De Leeuw, Penguin Books, 1965.

On the basis which consultation of these sources will give him the teacher can build as his experience in tutoring courses or his own research activities provide him with additional material.

B. Essential Requirements

The room should be an appropriate size for the group being instructed. Rooms which are too large or too small should be avoided as these have been found to hinder the development of an all-important informal group atmosphere. This is a small point, but one which is often overlooked, with noticeable effects on the results of courses.

Desks or tables should be arranged in a U-shape and a timing device with a minute hand and a large second hand should be positioned where all the students can see it easily. Ensure that each student has adequate stationery and writing materials.

Each student will need a copy of this book and it is also recommended that they each have a copy of *Reading Faster: a drill book* by Edward Fry for additional practice material.

C. Size of Groups

Fewer than six students limits fruitful discussion and more than fifteen becomes progressively more difficult to handle as an informal group. The best size seems to be in the region of ten to twelve students. All members of a group should be volunteers, although successful courses have been run with reluctant and sceptical groups of students.

D. Length of Course

The course should be extended over at least ten weeks, with at least one of the passages being read and discussed in class each week. If Dr Fry's book is also used, then it should be possible to occupy part of the time available for English or Liberal/General Studies over a whole academic year. This would have the advantage of permitting much more gradual progress and would also allow more time for encouraging students to develop new reading interests.

Weekly sessions should be between thirty minutes (for a one-year course) and two hours (for a ten-week course). Sessions shorter than two hours on the short course will mean that discussion will have to be limited.

Where possible, sessions should be held in the second half of the morning, though afternoon and evening sessions have been used with considerable success. However, sessions in the early evening, held soon after students have finished a day's work, should be avoided at all costs.

E. Methods of Teaching

There is no evidence to suggest that courses which employ visual and mechanical aids (pacers, films, teaching machines and the like) are any more effective than those which do not. It might, therefore, be wise to defer the purchase of any expensive equipment until the teacher is more familiar with the nature of efficient reading techniques and the particular needs of his own students. There is then a better chance of the most suitable equipment being obtained. At first, the progress graphs are the only visual aids that will be needed.

A simple combination of instruction, practice and discussion will be found effective with most groups. Only the more reluctant students will need the novelty of a film or a machine.

F. Optional Equipment Recommended

For those who decide, after consideration, that they would like their courses to be supported by visual and other aids, evaluations and recommendations on some films, pacers and teaching machines currently available can be found in *Efficiency in Reading: a report on courses run at the Hull College of Technology* by G. R. Wainwright, Dock Leaves Press.

The author will be pleased to supply teachers with the addresses of manufacturers and details of the cost of the equipment they produce.

G. A Suggested Scheme of Work

To aid teachers in the organization of material, a suggested scheme of work for a ten-week short course of two-hour sessions is given here:

1. Assessment of present reading speed and level of comprehension by reading Passage One in this book; introduction to the aims of the course, why reading efficiency courses are necessary; discussion of present reading problems experienced by students in the group.
2. Comparison of techniques used by slow and efficient readers; avoiding regressions.
3. Increasing eye span and speed of perception; purpose in reading; avoiding tension when reading 'against the clock'.
4. Developing anticipation skills in reading; improving concentration; rhythmic eye movements; skimming skills.
5. The principles of construction of written material; levels of difficulty in written material; flexibility in choice of reading technique.
6. Problems of particular kinds of material.
7. Methods of improving comprehension.
8. Principles of a critical approach to reading.
9. Techniques of reading for study purposes.
10. Assessment of present reading speed and comprehension by reading Passage Ten in this book; continuation work; course evaluation discussion.

H. Individual Tuition

Not only do students progress at different rates, they also experience individual problems in the process of improving their reading efficiency. One reason for limiting the size of groups is so that some time can be spent in giving individual advice. A further way in which this can be done is to use 'Record of Practice' forms which the students complete at the beginning of each meeting. At the close of each meeting, the teacher collects them in and returns them the following week with individual comments on progress.

I. Record of Practice Forms

These can be quite simple in construction. The following example has been used with success:

Record of Practice Form

1. *Practice*. State briefly:
   (a) the material you have used for practice ....
   ....
   (b) how long you have practised each day.......................
   (c) any problems you have encountered in your practice
   ....
   ....
   (d) how well *you* feel you are progressing ....
   ....

2. *Today's Results in Class*
   Reading Speed: .... words per minute.
   Comprehension: .... Retention: .... out of ten.
   Understanding and Interpretation: .... (A, B, C, D or E).
   Discussion and Evaluation: .... (A, B, C, D or E).

3. *Tutor's Comments* ....
   ....
   ....
   ....

J. Integration of Course

There is no reason why a reading efficiency training course should not be run as a separate, once-and-for-all short course. The main disadvantage is that improvements may not be permanent. For gains to be maintained a certain amount of continuation work is necessary and this is perhaps more likely to be achieved where the reading course forms a part of a one-year course in English or Liberal/General Studies. Some of the lines along which this integration can take place have already been indicated in the Introduction to this book.

This book and the scheme of work for a ten-week course suggested earlier are particularly well suited to forming a starting point for a one-year course, though a course can be placed at any point in the over all scheme of work that the teacher desires.

K. Continuation Work

The importance of follow-up testing and the provision of further practice and even 'booster' courses where students require them should be recognized. Some continuation work has already been suggested in the Introduction, but students should be encouraged to practice regularly on different kinds of reading material. The process of improvement lasts for much longer than ten weeks, or even a year. Frequent reference to reading efficiency and monthly reading tests help not only to persuade students of the importance of efficient reading habits, but also provide useful information on the short and long term effectiveness of the course.

In follow-up testing, care should be taken to see that the material used is comparable to that used in this book. Passages can be validated to some extent by inserting them into a course. If the results obtained on the material fit in with the pattern of results on previous and subsequent passages, then it would appear that they are sufficiently comparable to use them for follow-up testing. After all, results are not being measured with mathematical accuracy and a reasonable closeness in the level of difficulty is all most teachers will require.

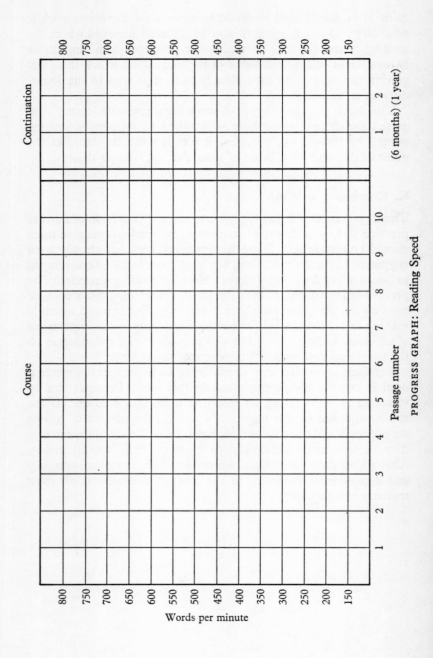

PROGRESS GRAPH: Reading Speed

Continuation

Course

Words per minute

800 750 700 650 600 550 500 450 400 350 300 250 200 150

Passage number

1 2 3 4 5 6 7 8 9 10 1 2

(6 months) (1 year)

88

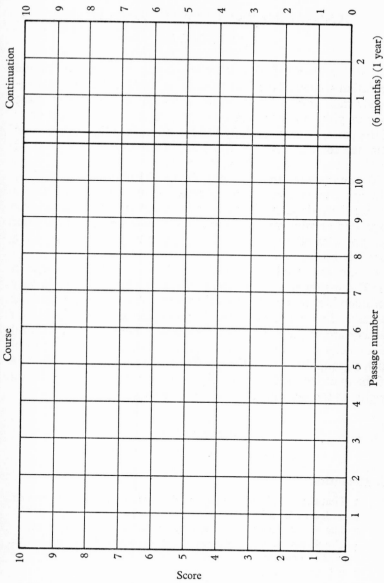

PROGRESS GRAPH: Retention (Answers to questions in Section A)

Continuation

Course

Passage number

(6 months) (1 year)

Score

ANSWERS TO COMPREHENSION QUESTIONS

You will probably find that your answers to questions in the Retention section of the Comprehension Tests will be either completely right or completely wrong. If you disagree with any of the answers given to Retention questions, re-read the relevant parts of the passages very carefully before you make a final decision on what the correct answer is. Answers need not be correct word for word, so long as the meaning is the same.

Your answers to the Understanding and Interpretation sections will not always agree with the answers suggested here. It is a matter for individual decision on whether to accept the answer suggested or your own. As you are only competing with yourself and not with others, you have everything to gain by considering carefully before deciding.

Comments have been offered on only some of the questions in the Discussion and Evaluation sections as answers here will vary considerably and many 'correct' answers are possible in a number of cases. Those who are using this book under the guidance of a teacher are in the most fortunate position here and many useful discussions should result. You will often find that, at the end of such a group discussion, the answers you would then give to some of the questions will be very different from those you considered 'right' at the beginning of the discussion.

Passage One

from *Communications* by Raymond Williams

A. Retention

1 That there is already a 'correct' form of modern English speech.
2 Both may be rejected.
3 The written report, memos, minutes, all letters, official forms.
4 The forms we are taught have little to do with actual writing we need to practise.
5 It is regarded as a form of play.
6 Poems, stories, plays, figures, pictures, models, music, dance.
7 The idea that education has done its work when it has introduced us to a few classic authors, such as Goldsmith.

8 Bring in creative artists and performers who can communicate the quality and the excitement of their own work.

9 Because of the spirit it communicates.

10 A separation between art and society.

B. Understanding and Interpretation

1 (a) Some of our teaching of communication and the practice and appreciation of the arts is hindered by assumptions taken over from old-fashioned ideas of culture and society and some of it is even harmful.

(b) The question of good speech is deeply confused and is in itself a major source of many of the divisions in our culture.

(c) Practice in speech and writing should be more closely related to the actual kinds we normally have to use.

(d) We should spend more time in the practice of all forms of creative expression throughout our education.

(e) The proper extension of creative practice is direct experience of all the contemporary arts at their best.

(f) Contact with creative artists and performers is important in developing understanding and appreciation of contemporary arts.

2 Constructively critical, but making insufficient acknowledgement to its present considerable achievements.

3 That we should re-think our approach to this kind of teaching and try to relate it more closely to students' needs and to the needs of modern society.

4 They are valuable and we should teach them—but the teaching of the arts should not stop there.

5 (a) The assumption that introducing us to such 'classic' writers as Goldsmith is as far as our education in the arts needs to go.

(b) The range of artistic works which give us our standards of evaluation and which are generally accepted as representing the best of artistic achievement through the ages.

(c) A collected artistic achievement and range of self-expression which can be appreciated by all regardless of educational or social background.

(d) Received Standard English, with especial reference in this connection to the kind of accent in speaking associated with those who have been educated at public schools and Oxbridge.

(e) The problem caused by trying to use one form of the English language (especially in speech) when communicating with others who are familiar with its regional characteristics and another form (Received Standard English) when communicating with those who are not familiar with, or prepared to accept, the first.

91

C. Discussion and Evaluation

4 There are many ways in which a critical evaluation can be executed, but for those who are uncertain as to how they should tackle this task, the following method of approach may be helpful:

Use the first reading of a passage to give you an over-view of the ideas, information and experiences it contains. Then consider four main aspects of the passage:

(a) Consider the information content of the material and ask yourself:

What exactly is the author telling me? What are the main points he makes?

Are his facts correct, so far as I can tell?

What is his authority for saying what he does?

(b) Consider the writer's intentions and ask yourself:

What is he trying to achieve? What are his purposes in saying what he does?

Are his aims 'honourable' ones or is the passage merely propaganda?

Am I being convinced by reason or emotion?

What evidence is there here of bias? or of selection of information to conceal truth?

Any evidence of deliberate distortion by the writer?

(c) Consider the treatment (find out how he has put his ideas across and you find out much about your acceptance or rejection of them) and ask yourself:

On what basis is the information selected?

What is the pattern of organization?

Within the organizational framework of the material how is the information arranged?

Is there anything in the above three questions that has unduly influenced me?—good presentation often hides a weak case.

What kind of style? Has this influenced me?

(d) Consider the degree of the writer's success (i.e. how far he has succeeded in saying what he wanted to say, in achieving his aims by saying it and in treating the material suitably and effectively):

What is my final judgement?

If the writer fails, how, why and in which parts particularly does he fail?

Passage Two

from *Straight and Crooked Thinking* by Robert Thouless

A. Retention

1 That the lunatic is a person suffering from a defect in his power of reasoning.
2 He holds some absurd belief.
3 That his beliefs are beginning to be threatened by our arguments.
4 Deliberately angering him so that we may take advantage of the fact that he will argue less efficiently in a condition of anger.
5 Be increasingly courteous to our opponent and increasingly critical of our own position.
6 Because of his desire for life.
7 On the side of preservation of the existing order.
8 Our childish love for our father or our resentment of his discipline.
9 Entirely rational grounds.
10 How far the irrational grounds on which it is based are hidden from our awareness.

B. Understanding and Interpretation

1 (a) We tend to think wrongly not so much because we *cannot* think straight as because of our prejudices.
  (b) Education does not in itself save us from having prejudices.
  (c) We are all prone to defend our prejudices by logical reasoning.
  (d) Though they may be defended rationally, our prejudices are based on emotional needs.
  (e) The way to conquer our prejudices is for us first to *realize* that they are based on irrational grounds.

2 We should examine our opinions closely and objectively to discover prejudice. We should base our opinions not so much on what we should like to believe as on what the fullest possible knowledge of the facts indicates we should believe. We shall only avoid holding prejudices rather than informed opinions if we are prepared to be completely honest with ourselves.

3 Opinions based on prejudices are worthless, for our colleagues and others will pay less attention to what we have to say unless their prejudices happen to coincide with ours. We therefore find it much more difficult to play an effective part in any discussion.

4 It ought to help us but it does not necessarily do so, perhaps because not many of us receive any training in self-analysis and straight thinking.

5 (a) An opinion based on emotion rather than reason.
  (b) Beliefs that situations imagined are in fact real.

(c) A person who holds an extreme opinion based on a prejudice.

(d) A statement about a subject put forward for discussion.

(e) The way in which society is organized and controlled at present.

C. Discussion and Evaluation

1 Base your answer not so much on your own education as on the kind of education that you think people generally receive. Any prejudice in your assessment of this?

3 This question needs answering particularly carefully as it is often suggested that we do not need to be clear and logical in our thinking for everyday conversational purposes.

5 Refer back to C4 on Passage One for a comment on this.

Passage Three

from *The True Believer* by Eric Hoffer

A. Retention

1 That there can be no new beginning as long as the old clutters the landscape.

2 To lose individuality in the grandeur of a mighty whole.

3 The non-creative men of words.

4 Those who can find fulfilment in creative work and those who cannot.

5 Refer back to the passage for the answer to this question.

6 Music.

7 It saps his creative energies.

8 He cannot settle down.

9 They make enemies of one another.

10 The entrance of a practical man of action.

B. Understanding and Interpretation

1 They are necessary for progress but must be controlled.

2 These lie in the degree of fulfilment from creative work and in the use of critical faculties.

3 The fanatic is essentially an anarchist.

4 No, because of his fanaticism.

5 Lenin. The stability (i.e. durability) of Russian society since the revolution.

Passage Four

from *Six Days or Forever?* by Ray Ginger

A. Retention

1 Prosecution—William Jennings Bryan.
  Defence—Clarence Darrow.
2 The Butler Act.
3 'I believe in a God who can make a whale and can make a man and make both do what he pleases.'
4 The legal shrewdness of forcing a leader of the prosecution to admit that the Bible must be interpreted, the glee to be found in exposing a fanatic, the exquisite pleasure that any craftsman finds in using his tools, his anger with Bryan.
5 9 a.m. on 23 October 4004 B.C.
6 By hearsay, what other people had told him.
7 'Not six days of twenty-four hours.'
8 Fundamentalists.
9 Millions of years.
10 A day of reversals.

B. Understanding and Interpretation

1 Bryan's 'Not six days of twenty-four hours'.
2 Bryan would not answer a question directly.
3 That the Bible must be interpreted and cannot be accepted literally.
4 To establish Bryan's authority for leading the prosecution so that his discrediting of Bryan (if he were able to achieve it) would have greater impact.
5 (*a*) Braces.
  (*b*) Helped to compensate him for.
  (*c*) Rambling.
  (*d*) Having eyes like a pig's.
  (*e*) Summoning to appear in court.

C. Discussion and Evaluation

1 It is advisable to read Passage Three again quickly but carefully before attempting to discuss this question.
3 In discussing this question, you need not necessarily restrict yourself to restrictions on the teaching of religion.
4 You can check the jury's actual decision in this case by reading *Six Days or Forever?* by Ray Ginger or the play *Inherit the Wind* by Jerome Lawrence and Robert E. Lee. You should also see the film *Inherit the Wind* if possible.

Passage Five

from *The Guardian*: 'Not So Simple as ABC' by G. R. Wainwright

A. Retention

1 They simply cannot read quickly enough.
2 The United States.
3 In the mid-1950s.
4 None.
5 An analysis of the skills used by naturally efficient readers.
6 The efficient reader's generally wider and more thoughtful approach to knowledge and experience.
7 An increase in reading speed of well over 100 per cent and an improvement in comprehension of over 25 per cent.
8 Refer to the passage for the answer to this question.
9 Half.
10 One is trying to change habits of several years' duration and the course merely shows how to begin the process of improvement.

B. Understanding and Interpretation

1 They do not move smoothly along the lines, but move in a series of jerks, stopping momentarily to 'read' at each fixation point. Slower readers' eyes regress (go back to a previous fixation) more often than faster readers' eyes.

2	*Poor Readers*	*Efficient Readers*
(1)	Read slowly.	Read faster, generally speaking.
(2)	Regress.	Do not regress so often.
(3)	Narrow span of perception.	Wider span of perception.
(4)	Subvocalize.	Tend not to subvocalize.
(5)	Limited vocabulary.	Wider vocabulary.
(6)	Poor concentration.	Better concentration.
(7)	Irregular eye movements.	Rhythmic reading sweep.
(8)	Poor anticipation.	Good anticipation.
(9)	Lack purpose.	Clear knowlege of purpose.
(10)	Narrow and less thoughtful approach to knowledge and experience.	Wider and more thoughtful approach to knowledge and experience.

3 No; one of the reasons for the introduction of courses was to improve comprehension and results support the view that comprehension tends to improve.
4 There is more in one's approach and attitude to reading than a concern for speed or comprehension. In the modern world of the mass media teachers are anxious to encourage people to be

96

more *interested* in reading because reading is more than a method of acquiring information, it is a liberalizing and a cultural influence.

5 (*a*) Combining speed with accuracy.
  (*b*) Understanding.
  (*c*) A keen reader, one who reads a great deal and enjoys reading.
  (*d*) Read 'aloud' silently.
  (*e*) Becoming an efficient reader in a very short time without much instruction, effort or practice (which is an impossibility).

Passage Six

from *How To Study* by Harry Maddox

A. Retention

1 Survey, Question, Read, Recite, Revise.
2 Slow and thorough.
3 You will often miss major points the author is trying to make.
4 Bacon.
5 Outlining the substance of a passage.
6 When memorizing formulae, foreign language vocabularies, anatomical facts.
7 Survey.
8 After reading each major section of a chapter.
9 Two years.
10 Herbart.

B. Understanding and Interpretation

1 The habit of asking questions, looking for evidence for statements, judging whether what one has read is consistent with one's previous experience or not.
2 No. It is of value but it may be of little use in the early stages of learning and nothing should ever be learned as an isolated, meaningless unit.
3 Memories become stronger and stronger with each re-learning, and forgetting proceeds more slowly; computers can 'remember' permanently after only one 'input'.
4 The science student because of the usually high pass mark (near 100 per cent in medicine, for example). Arts studies are not subject to the same kind of 'life or death' standards, nor do they usually deal with skills or the acquisition of large amounts of factual information.
5 The latter.

C. Discussion and Evaluation

1 Among the other kinds of reading you may like to consider are: reading for general information; proof-reading; reading in order to analyse and evaluate; reading in order to reach a decision (i.e. when reading correspondence, reports, memos, etc.); reading for enjoyment; students' background reading (journals, books that are not prescribed textbooks, etc.).

Passage Seven

from *Personal Values in the Modern World* by M. V. C. Jeffreys

A. Retention

1 Effective communication among its members.
2 The enormous development of the technical means of communication (the mass media); the fact that our national and international problems increasingly depend for their solution on effective communication.
3 The Iron Curtain.
4 The virtual disappearance of the old mixed community of the village or market town.
5 To encourage creative work that will reach the general public.
6 The modern intellectual.
7 Fiction and drama which are analytic rather than constructive, negative rather than positive, depressive rather than inspiring.
8 Shared feeling.
9 Experience approached sensitively.
10 It loses value and significance as an electric battery runs down.

B. Understanding and Interpretation

1 (*a*) A society cannot have a coherent culture unless there is effective communication among its members.
  (*b*) The role of the intellectual in developing a coherent culture is restricted by his failure to communicate more generally and he must overcome this.
  (*c*) The basis of communication is shared feeling and we must communicate more, therefore, through the common elements in our experience.
  (*d*) Experience is wider and more common than language and helps promote personal relationships.
  (*e*) True communication is personal and we must therefore promote relationships between people at a truly personal level.
2 (*a*) So involved in their own special interests that they are unaware of how the rest of us think and feel.

98

(b) Make intelligible to the general public, usually by simplifying.

(c) One whose opinions are ahead of the current commonly held opinions on any subject.

(d) Authority, those who occupy positions which enable them to exercise some control over the progress of national affairs.

(e) People must first have something in common before they can begin to understand each other.

3 (a) They are not inherently harmful but could be much more wisely used.

(b) They could be much more useful to society if they would learn to 'communicate'.

(c) Its impersonal character is doing great harm to personal relationships.

(d) It has an important part to play in improving the quality of life.

4 Because of his religious attachments and because they promote communication.

5 Because it will lead to better personal relationships which will lead to higher standards of personal values.

Passage Eight

from *Discrimination and Popular Culture* edited by Denys Thompson

A. Retention

1 Town crier, notice in church porch, back-street printer.
2 That workers who became literate would give themselves a liberal education.
3 Mass production.
4 £150,000.
5 Quantity becomes more important than quality.
6 They are indifferent, stupid and uninterested in education of any kind.
7 It distorts a nation's economy.
8 A form of propaganda for things as they are.
9 Hostile.
10 Schools are still organized to prepare entrants to industry instead of providing education for life.

B. Understanding and Interpretation

1 They are an anti-educative force in our society.
2 The quality of each might improve.
3 Mass production, even in the mass media, pays better when millions are satisfied than when only a few are.

4 The teaching of how to use reading skills effectively should be continued throughout compulsory secondary education; young people should be encouraged to be more critical in their acceptance of the printed word.

5 (a) Education concerned with a deeper understanding of the arts, humanities and sciences than can be provided within the limited context of vocational training.

(b) So many people have a *part* to play in producing even a single piece of entertainment that no one really feels much responsibility for the *whole* product.

(c) Things which demand no effort of the intellect to understand or appreciate.

(d) Entertainment which is not motivated in any way to do anything more than please its spectators.

(e) Other people's attitudes and opinions mould our own and vice versa so that each individual's personality is very much a reflection of many others.

Passage Nine

from *The Listener*: 'The BBC's Duty to Society' by Sir Hugh Greene

A. Retention

1 To make the microphone and the TV screen available to the widest possible range of subjects and to the best exponents available of the differing views on any given subject.

2 One of healthy scepticism.

3 Royal Charter; licence from the Postmaster General.

4 Broadcast a daily account of Parliament's proceedings.

5 Its own self-control and the laws of the country.

6 Senior clergy, writers of leading articles in newspapers, presidents of national voluntary organizations.

7 Ordinary decent people.

8 Henrik Ibsen.

9 Words 'gas chamber' being deleted from play (*Judgment at Nuremberg*) sponsored by the U.S. gas industry.

10 Where there are clashes for or against the basic moral values; issues like racialism and extreme forms of political belief.

B. Understanding and Interpretation

1 He thinks they are socially dangerous and that they should not be allowed to influence our decisions on what should or should not be broadcast.

2 (a) Requiring to be convinced by sound arguments and reliable evidence before forming an opinion.

(b) To gain people's co-operation in doing or not doing something in preference to telling them categorically what they must or must not do.

(c) People who share their opinions and whom they suppose to be the mass of the population.

(d) One which springs spontaneously out of public opinion.

(e) With the lack of bias or favour for one side or the other required by law.

3 He considers that present controls are sufficient and is opposed to further forms of censorship.

4 They want broadcasting to confine itself to the generally acceptable, innocuous and safe (and therefore dull and ultra-conservative).

5 The new populists.

C. Discussion and Evaluation

2 Before attempting to answer this you should read the BBC and ITA charters and the Report of the Pilkington Committee on The Future of Broadcasting.

Passage Ten

from *Communications* by Raymond Williams

A. Retention

1 Their history, how they work, their current social organization (any of these qualifies as an answer).

2 His experience of radio and TV production and of publishing.

3 A dull and inert 'appreciation'.

4 That once you know the good you can distinguish the bad.

5 Refer to the passage for the answer to this question.

6 Adults and young workers.

7 Supply catalogues; collect and prepare new material, particularly in visual fields (either qualifies as an answer).

8 It would undertake long-range research and analysis at university level.

9 In adolescence.

10 Teachers and educational administrators.

B. Understanding and Interpretation

1 (a) Because of the importance the institutions of communication now have in our society, we should include the teaching of certain basic facts about them in all our education.

(b) Education should be critical of all cultural work, but the criticism should be based on personal practice and experience.

(c) We must be prepared to look at the bad work as well as the good and we should include 'the world of ordinary communication' in our teaching of criticism.

(d) Teachers should be offered training in this kind of work and communications research and information services should be set up to support this work.

(e) This work is sufficiently important to make time for it in school and college curricula, especially for adolescents.

(f) Educationists and responsible people in communications should work as closely as possible with each other.

2 He thinks that they are partly right but they must make a real effort to co-operate rather than conflict with those who operate the mass media.

3 That we shall need in the future to devote much more time and attention to the study of the media of communication if we are to ensure that they serve us in our own best interests and do not merely give us what *they* consider 'the public wants'.

4 We are often not sufficiently critical.

5 (a) An attractive presentation designed to create a favourable impression.

(b) The products of the modern mass media of communication.

(c) Commonly held and usually mistaken impressions of what people, jobs, etc., are really like.

(d) Attitudes and standards of behaviour expected in school and those permitted outside.

(e) A public which has a respect for knowledge and wants to use it wisely.